eat.shop portland

**fifth edition : researched, photographed and written by
kaie wellman and jon hart**

cabazon books : 2008

table of contents

eat

shop

kaie's + jon's notes on portland

k: i'm glad jon talks about the rain below, so now i don't have to. being a native portlander, i've got nothing more to say on the topic other than: the moistness here is good for the skin. so i guess this leaves me to talk about this book. it's the fifth edition of *eat.shop portland*. wow. over 400 homegrown bizs have appeared in this guide over the last five years. that gives me the tingles. even better, most of these businesses are still open and as vibrant as the day they originally opened. sure, doors have closed over the years—but the majority have stayed open. portlanders should be chuffed.

i'm guessing in the next couple of years that we all will be keeping closer watch on our pocketbooks. but i am here to encourage that when there's spending to be done, whether it be eating or shopping, that it be done locally. you don't need the speech, so i won't give it. but i will say that the over 400 businesses that have been featured over the years in this guide are incredible. and your dollar is happier being spent on incredible.

. . . .

j: for years i have tried to pinpoint what makes this odd / awesome city so great. portland is not the only city with inspiring natural beauty, access to outstanding farm-raised foods, and world-class arts and culture. something sets us apart. i think it's the rain. our six month rhythm of lightness (some sun, high clouds, some warmth), then darkness (no sun, lots of clouds, very little warmth) seems to attract a certain type of person. in fact, i consider the rainy season here to be a citywide physical fitness test, weeding out the weak and feeble, leaving behind a strong stock willing to enjoy the full spectrum of emotions that a lack of sun brings. it breeds a young artistic pioneering spirit—a person willing to visit the depths of despair in february, weeping over something as simple as a shoelace becoming untied in return for the euphoria of riding a bike through a flurry of pink cherry blossoms set afloat by a pleasant april breeze.

i love the rain. it's what attracted me to move here 15 years ago. i'll admit that come june i grumble about it a little, but that is all a part of the pdx story. you can call me old fashioned or priggish, but i think you need the good with the bad, joy and melancholy, to have balance and appreciate greatness. whatever it is, i am just happy to have this... portland.

23 hoyt

sophisticated atmosphere, comforting food

529 northwest 23rd avenue. corner of hoyt
503.445.7400 www.23hoyt.com
tue - sat 5p - late

opened in 2006. owner: bruce carey chef: chris israel
$$ - $$$: all major credit cards accepted
dinner. full bar. reservations recommended

northwest : nob hill > **e01**

J: You know the game "Six Degrees of Kevin Bacon" where most actors can be tracked back to Mr. Bacon? In the Portland restaurant world, it's the "Three Degrees of Bruce Carey." Nearly all of the great local restaurants that have popped up in the last five years can trace their roots back to one of his famed places—Zefiro, Bluehour and Saucebox. It is no surprise, then, that with *23 Hoyt* he again hits all of the marks: sophisticated, yet comforting cuisine, killer cocktails, modern interiors and impeccable service. Bruce has the magic touch.

imbibe / *devour:*
the arboretum
zefiro martini
gnocchi alle erbette
grilled spot prawns with romesco
sautéed idaho trout with horseradish cream
lamb shank printanier
späetzle with braised rabbit, leeks & morels
butterscotch pots de crème

alba osteria & enoteca

the cooking of piemonte

6440 southwest capitol highway. just west of bertha blvd
503.977.3045 www.albaosteria.com
tue - thu, sun 5:30 - 9p fri - sat 5:30 - 9:30p

opened in 2003. owner/chef: kurt spak
$$ - $$$: all major credit cards accepted
dinner. reservations accepted

southwest : hillsdale >

K: I have a special affinity for the Piemonte region of Italy. It's here that I fell in love, it's here that I was married, and it's here that I dream of when I think about Italian food. When most Americans think about Italian cuisine, they think about dishes influenced by southern Italy. But up north—in the towns of Barbaresco, Barolo and Alba—the food is lighter and dominated by red sauces. *Alba*, the restaurant, offers up some of my favorite Piemontese dishes like carne cruda, which is akin to steak tartare, and pastas like tajarin dressed simply with butter and sage. *Grazie.*

imbibe / devour:
deltetto brut rosé
cantino del pino ovello
carne cruda
jerusalem artichokes baked in bagna cauda
tajarin with butter & sage
agnolotti dal plin filled with veal, pork & rabbit
crepinette with umbrian lental
torta noccioli with zabaglione

alu

wine bar and lounge with exceptional german cuisine

2831 northeast martin luther king boulevard. between graham and stanton
503.258.9463 www.alupdx.com
tue - thu 4p - midnight fri - sat 4p - 1a

opened in 2008. owner: paul wagner chef: sandro di giovani
$ - $$: all major credit cards accepted
dinner. full bar. first come, first served

northeast : mlk > **e03**

J: Acronyms are popular these days. Everyone is using gems like OMG, MILF or WWJD. Friends and I always try to start new ones. CUS stands for constant upgrade syndrome, coined for a friend in perpetual need of fancier things. Another useful nugget is AWAKC—amazing wine and killer cuisine. The perfect example of this is *Alu*. The wine offerings are choice, and you'd be a fool to not embrace Chef Sandro's incredible German specialties. Oh, just thought of another one. SIPPY—spätzle is perfect with pinot, yummy.

imbibe / devour:
wachtenburg winzer grauburgunder
foundry vineyards cabernet sauvignon
zwiebelkuchen
roasted beet, cucumber & tangelo salad
maultaschen with brown butter
käsespätzle
duck confit, spinach, & hammy lentils
german apple & rum custard pie

bar mingo

simple italian

811 northwest 21st avenue. between johnson and kearney
503.455.4646 www.caffemingonw.com
daily 4p - midnight

opened in 2008. owners: michael cronan and joe cleary chef: jerry huisinga
$$: all major credit cards accepted
dinner. full bar (this is a 21 + only establishment) first come, first served

northwest : nob hill > **e04**

K: Everybody has a favorite restaurant. A place that trumps all others when it comes to eating out because you really feel like it's your place. *Caffé Mingo* holds this title for many people I know, and for many years. Recently though, the folks at *Mingo* have thrown a curveball to their adoring followers. They opened the sexy *Bar Mingo* next to the *Caffé*. It was packed from day one. So, which to pick? The small plate concept at the *Bar* or their beloved *Caffé*? Oh, the divine torture. I suggest alternating on a weekly (or daily if you wish) basis.

imbibe / devour:
bellini
negroni
seafood salad
bresaola
suppli al telefono
tonnarelli
swordfish rotolo
profiteroles

beast

six-course dinners in an intimate kitchen setting
5425 northeast 30th avenue. between killingsworth and emerson
503.841.6968 www.beastpdx.com
wed - sat 5:30 - 9:30p sat - sun 11a - 2p

opened in 2007. owner: mika paredes chef: naomi pomeroy
$$ - $$$: mc. visa
dinner. brunch. wine / beer. reservations recommended

northeast : alberta > **e05**

J: Kaie and I are always trying to make each other cry (in a schmaltzy, romance movie type of way). Perhaps we anticipated needing each other visiting *Beast* for the first time. We were well aware of the sublime quality of Naomi's food, but a six course, prix fixe menu was a whole new ball game. Thank god Kaie was there to wipe the tear that fell as I tasted the veal consommé, its flavors so deep, yet delicate. And I was glad to help Kaie when she got choked up over the foie gras bonbon. We finished our rhubarb shortcake in each other's arms, sobbing with the deliciousness of it all.

imbibe / devour:
nigl piri gruner veltliner
brundlmayer riesling
veal consommé, english pea toasts & quail egg
charcuterie plate with foie gras bonbons
venison medallion with morels & white asparagus
wild greens, ramps & sage fried prosciutto
fraga raw goat cheddar
rhubarb shortcake with buttermilk ice cream

belmont station

specialty and craft beer store

4500 southeast stark street. corner of 45th
503.232.8538 www.belmont-station.com
mon - sat 10a - 10p sun noon - 8p (café open later)

opened in 1997. owner: carl singmaster
$ - $$: mc. visa
lunch. grocery. wine / beer only. first come, first served

southeast : sunnyside > **e06**

J: The *eat.shop guides* were started, in part, to educate folks about Portland because a decade ago many out-of-towners only knew of our rain and beer culture. Nowadays the *New York Times* snogs Portland weekly with its raves on the city's food and wine. So I'm here to remind you what got Portland put on the map in the first place—beer! This city has the most microbreweries per capita pumping out amazing ales and porters. And *Belmont Station* is the best place to find said libations. Whether it is a small-production, local lager or a super specialty Belgian ale, this place has it all.

imbibe / devour:
oregon trail bourbon porter from oregon
cascade lakes monkey face porter from oregon
anderson valley tripel from california
fantôme la dalmatienne from belgium
bfm cuvèe du 7éme from switzerland
brouwerij de regenboog guido from belgium
hobnobs (nobbly, oaty biscuits) from england
good food in the café

biwa

authentic japanese yakimono and noodles

215 southeast ninth avenue. corner of ash
503.239.8830 www.biwarestaurant.com
mon - thu 5 - 10p fri - sat 5 - 11p

opened in 2007. owner / chef: gabe rosen
$ - $$: mc. visa
dinner. full bar. reservations accepted for parties of six or more

southeast : industrial > **e07**

J: My two ultimate comfort foods are soup and noodles, so nothing is more nurturing than a visit to *Biwa*. A steaming bowl of dark and salty pork broth with handmade ramen topped with pork loin, bbq pork, and bacon may sound like a lot of pig parts—but this I believe is the reason the Japanese live longer than Americans. *Biwa* features other Japanese classics like yakimono (grilled skewers) and killer handmade gyoza, too. But the next time Portland has experienced its 20th consecutive day of rain, look for me here, slurping a bowl of ramen, getting my groove back.

imbibe / devour:
yuki no bosha junmai ginjo sake
geisha party cocktail
tsukemono (japanese pickles)
salmon tataki
udon nabeyaki
pork "bara" belly
hiya yakko soft tofu
green tea ice cream

blueplate

lunch counter and soda fountain

308 southwest washington street. between third and fourth
503.295.2583 www.eatatblueplate.com
mon - fri 10a - 5p

opened in 2006. owner / chef: jeffery reiter
$$: all major credit cards accepted
lunch. early dinner. first come, first served

southwest : downtown > 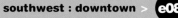 **e08**

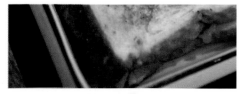

K : As a parent, I admit, I am not above using bribery every now and then (or daily). And nothing works better than a big ole, three-scoop ice cream sundae eaten sitting on swivel stools at an old-school-esque soda fountain, feet dangling. This is the experience at *Blueplate*. When they catch a whiff of the sliders (mini hamburgers) on the grill and see the creamy milkshakes (made with divine Cascade Glacier ice cream) being blended, your kids will be putty in your hands. The hamster cage that hasn't been cleaned for six months will soon be sparkling.

imbibe / devour:
egg cream
tooted fruit soda
grilled cheese & tomato soup
northwest sliders
blt salad
knife & fork chili dog
sundaes!!!
classic banana split

broder

ultra cute swedish café

2508 southeast clinton street. between 25th and 26th
503.736.3333
mon - sun 9a - 2p dinner thu - sat 5:30 - 10:30p

opened in 2007. owner: peter bro chefs: j.j. needhma and alton garcia
$$: mc. visa
breakfast. lunch. dinner. full bar. reservations recommended

southeast : clinton >

J: My first introduction to Swedish food was through the Muppets. I loved the way the Swedish chef would throw food around while singing his gibberish song. It wasn't until later in life that I traveled to Sweden and learned the true joys of the cuisine, which can also be found at the adorable *Broder*. Scandinavian classics like Swedish meatballs are served alongside "bords" featuring meats, eggs, cheeses and breads. And I promise you will love life more if you partake in an aquavit along with your meal. And don't forget to hum the Swedish chef song, "de umn, børk! børk! børk!"

imbibe / devour:
op anderson aquavit
kölsch beer
pytt i panna (swedish hash)
broder club
baked scramble with smoked trout & red onion
three-course smorgasbord
meatball sandwich
aebleskiver (danish pancakes)

castagna / café castagna

modern european cuisine and bistro

1752 southeast hawthorne boulevard. (café castagna is next door). corner of 18th
res: 503.231.7373 café: 503.231.9959 www.castagnarestaurant.com
res: wed - sat 5:30p - close
cafe: lunch mon - fri 11:30a - 2p dinner 5:30p - close

opened in 1999. owners: monique siu and kevin gibson chef: elias cairo
$$ - $$$: all major credit cards accepted
lunch (café only). dinner. full bar. reservations accepted for parties of four or more

southeast : hawthorne >

K: This past Christmas, Jon and I and our respective significant others hosted a holiday dinner for friends at *Castagna*. For this evening to be described as anything less than magical would be a downright lie. The room sparkled and the wine flowed, exclamations were made over the meal and lo and behold, carols were sung—we had imbibed enough to convince ourselves we sounded angelic. Sober or soused, winter or summer, restaurant or café—*Castagna* is always memorable.

imbibe / devour:
elderflower cocktail
chilled asparagus soup with crème fraîche
house-cured anchovies with crostini
spinach, nettles & sheep's cheese calzone
proper bangers & mash with english peas
roasted black cod, varnish clams & fideos
the three-course menu in the restaurant
almond cake with poached apricots

cava

cozy neighborhood bistro
5339 southeast foster road. between 52nd and 54th
503.206.8615 www.cavapdx.com
wed - mon 5 - 10p

opened in 2007. owner: randy montgomery chef: j.b. tranholm
$ - $$: mc. visa
dinner. full bar. reservations accepted for parties of six or more

southeast : foster > **e11**

J: Eating at restaurants for a living rocks. And sometimes I like a place so much, I conspire to return immediately. *Cava* is a good example of this. The first time I went there, my photos didn't pass muster with Kaie, and she accused me of shooting while drinking. I feigned innocence and coyly said I would return. Success! The food is top notch here, yet not over the top. The atmosphere is comfortable, cheerful and neighborhoody. And owner Randy makes the most delicious rye manhattans. Oh dear, maybe Kaie was right.

imbibe / devour:
argento pink prosecco
cava cocktail
grilled polenta, grilled scallions & romesco
moroccan spiced roast chicken with onions
semolina gnocchi in tomato sauce
chimayo chile-rubbed, pulled-pork sandwich
grilled hangar steak with maitre d'hôtel butter
mocha brownie sundae

clyde common

domestic and foreign cooking

1014 southwest stark street. between 10th and 11th
503.228.3333 www.clydecommon.com
mon - thu 11:30a - midnight fri 11:30a - 2a sat 5p - 2a sun 5 - 10p

opened in 2007. owner: nate tilden chef: jason barwikowski
$$: all major credit cards accepted
lunch. dinner. reservations recommended

southwest : west end >

K: There are many things that I could tell you I love about *Clyde Common*: the soaring ceilings, the rollicking vibe, the simple-with-a-twist food. Yes, I could focus on all that, but what I really love is that with a minimum purchase of 50 bucks here, you can score a room at the adjoining Ace Hotel for the same night (*for $75 more and if a room's available of course). So I'll just order a coupla drinks, some of the addictive house popcorn, and two or three other items… and thank you very much, I'll take a room. Walking to the car will upset the balance of my perfectly satiated self…

imbibe / devour:
house lavender soda
popcorn & pimenton
the meatboard
scallop crudo, blood sausage & grapefruit
tagliatelle, stinging nettles & walnuts
grilled rabbit, watercress & wild mushrooms
caramel-pinenut tart
a room at the ace*

coffeehouse northwest

perfectly pulled coffee
1951 west burnside. corner of trinity place
503.248.2133 www.coffeehousenorthwest.com
mon - fri 7:30a - 7p sat - sun 7a - 7p

opened in 2005. owner: adam mcgovern
$: all major credit cards accepted
coffee / tea. first come, first served

northwest : lower nob hill >

J: I had heard what a master barista Adam was before going to *Coffeehouse Northwest*. So I was prepared to be impressed by his coffee pulling abilities. Watching his deliberate movements as he produced perfect latte after perfect macchiato for the community of northwest Portland coffee aficionados, I could tell he was an expert. On a rare breather between orders, he came over to talk to me as I sat taking pictures of his flawless beverages. "Have a hot chocolate," he knowingly suggested. He brought me a cup. Holy crap. I wasn't prepared for this. I bow to the master.

imbibe / devour:
perfect coffee
white mocha
amazing hot chocolate
wenshan baozhong oolong tea
monkey king green tea
yerba mate
fresh granola
anzac biscuits

cool moon ice cream

homemade ice cream by the best fountain in portland

1105 northwest johnson street. corner of 11th
503.224.2021 www.coolmoonicecream.com
tue - thu, sun noon - 10p fri - sat 10a - 11p

opened in 2007. owner: eva bernhard
$: mc. visa
treats. first come, first served

northwest : pearl district > **e14**

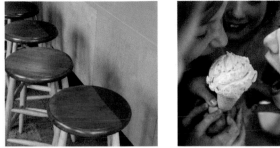

K: On a hot day in Portland, have you ever noticed that there don't seem to be any kids around? That's because the entire under-six population is at Jamison Square's fountain, racing around like banshees. But for me there's always been something missing in this area. Duh. Ice cream. Then *Cool Moon* opened across the street. Hurrah! They make their own ice cream. Hurrah squared! And for some real fun, take a small horde of water-logged kids here and plop a Real McCall sundae (11 scoops of ice cream, oh my!) in front of them. Then back away…

imbibe / devour:
dark moon hot chocolate
black cherry blues float
cyde & millie float
mexican chocolate shake
the real mccall sundae
caramelized sugar sundae
chocolate-covered frozen bananas
ice cream cakes

dove vivi

cornmeal crust pizza

2727 northeast glisan street. corner of 28th
503.239.4444 www.dovevivipizza.com
daily 4 - 10p

opened in 2007. owners / chefs: delane hamik and gavin blackstock
$ - $$: mc. visa
lunch. dinner. wine / beer only. reservations accepted for parties of six or more

northeast : east burnside > **e15**

J: Transformed from what might have once been a convenience store (though there is one still next door), the charming *Dove Vivi* serves up fantastic cornmeal crust pizza. Inspired by a famous San Francisco pizzeria, this is not your typical Dominos shlop. What makes the pie unique here is its deep-dish style and signature cornmeal crunch. Throw in unique california-esque toppings like smoked mozzarella and corn, and you've got some good eatin'. And convenient for an after party—just stop by next door to pick up a six of Bud after you're done.

imbibe / devour:
delirium tremens from huyghe brewery
ninkasi total domination ipa
broccoli, black bean & mushroom salad
pizza:
   roasted eggplant, mozzarella & blue cheese
   corn, smoked mozzarella & roasted onion
   pepperoni classico
homemade zuccotto

flavourspot

waffles and coffee cart
#1 cart: 2310 north lombard street. between boston and omaha
#2 cart: mississippi at fremont
503.289.9866 www.flavourspot.com
#1: mon - fri 6:30a - 3p sat - sun 8a - 3p / #2: weekends only 9a - 3p

opened in 2006. owner: david stokamer
$: cash
breakfast. lunch. first come, first served

north : st. johns / mississippi > **e16**

J: A beloved pastime for me is brainstorming ideas for businesses. *Donut Taste Delicious?* was a donut cart I never opened. Or the online social networking startup for the absentmided called *Mysplace*. I think *Flavourspot* was born out of such brainstorming. The idea: fresh waffles made into sandwiches, sold from a cart. In theory you might think, hmm... this is not going to work. But it does: a crisp waffle is the perfect housing for sandwich fixin's like the thb (turkey, havarti and bacon). In fact, this idea has worked so well there is a new weekend *Flavourspot* on Mississippi.

imbibe / devour:
vanilla fizz
maltball mocha
waffles:
  the mb9
  the thb
  sausage & maple waffle
  sweet cream and jam waffle
  s'more waffle with mallow fluff & nutella

fuller's coffee shop

classic portland diner

136 northwest ninth avenue. corner of davis

503.222.5608

mon - fri 6a - 3p sat 7a - 2p sun 8a - 2p

opened in 1941. owner: john fuller

$: cash

breakfast. lunch. first come, first served

northwest : pearl district > e17

K: Here is my ode to *Fuller's*: I love your little cans of tomato juice. I love your super-friendly wait staff (Susie, you're at the top of the list). I love your pancakes that you make into dollar sizes for Lola. I love your red swivel vinyl stools. I love your perfectly crunchy, always golden, hashbrowns. I love that you don't laugh at me when I ask for an American cheese omelet. I love the steam on the windows on cold days. I love your display of Lifesavers by the door. I love you because you are old Portland and you're steadfast and true and a downright classic.

imbibe / devour:
fresh strawberry shake
pig in a blanket
georgia's potato deluxe
fuller's famous omelet
breakfast steak
fuller's sloppy joe
club sandwich
homemade pie

garden state

sicilian-inspired food cart
next to 7875 southeast 13th avenue. corner of lexington
503.705.5273 www.gardenstatecart.com
wed - sun 11a - 3:30p

opened in 2007. owner / chef: kevin sandri
$: cash
lunch. early dinner. first come, first served

southeast : sellwood > **e18**

K: There have always been food carts, but in the last couple of years, they starte to pop up on foodie radar. Whether or not you follow, or care about, food trends— you will care about (deeply, I would guess) *Garden State*. Kevin is making some de-lish food here inspired by his Sicilian roots. The arancine are brilliant: savory morsels made with saffron rice, oozing cheese and an asparagus surprise in the middle. But what people line up for is the meatball hero. I could go into blathering detail, but I won't, because what needs to be said is that it's meaty bliss on a bun.

imbibe / devour:
cold san pellegrino aranciata
meatball hero
chickpea sandwich
sicilian fritelle:
 arancine
 cazilli
 panelle

hiroshi

glorious japanese cuisine

926 northwest tenth avenue. corner of glisan
503.619.0580
lunch tue - fri 11:30a - 2p dinner mon - thu 6:30 - 9:30p fri - sat 6:30 - 10p

opened in 2006. owner / chef: hiro ikegaya
$$ - $$$: all major credit cards accepted
lunch. dinner. reservations recommended
reservations accepted at the sushi bar only until seven

northwest : pearl district >

K: For years, I felt that sushi could do no wrong, and I embraced the westernization of the cuisine. California Roll? Yes, please. Dragon Spider Rock and Roll? Why not. But finally the names and the ingredients got too silly. Cream cheese, jalapeños and surimi? Ridiculous. I find now that I want purity and simplicity, and I want someone masterful to craft the food. If you feel the same, *Hiroshi* is for you. Hiro is brilliant, and I don't just suggest—but demand that you put yourself in his hands at the sushi bar and request omakase (chef's choice). The experience is sublime.

imbibe / devour:
yuki no bosha junmai ginjo cold sake
harushika diaginjo sake wine
omakase
uni & northern japan scallops ravioli style
hamachi daikon
grilled monkfish liver, caramelized pineapple,
   balsamic reduction & chive oil
scallop, salmon & tuna with a sumiso olive oil

41

hot pot city

taiwanese hot pot

1975 southwest first avenue, suite j. between lincoln and harrison
503.224.6696
mon - sun 11:30a - 9:30p

opened in 2002. owners: ruby and lu tsai
$ - $$: mc. visa
lunch. dinner. first come, first served

southwest : downtown >

J: Discovering new places while doing these guides is expected, but never before have I discovered an entire city. A tip from a friend led me just south of downtown to *Hot Pot City*. Though it doesn't have its own zip code, this place is far removed from the typical downtown eateries. And it is the only Taiwanese hot pot restaurant in town. Say what? A hot pot restaurant is like a buffet, but for soup, and you can pick your own ingredients which you then cook yourself from your own pot of bubbling tasty broth. I now count *Hot Pot City* as one of my new favorite cities.

imbibe / devour:
coca cola
spicy hot pot buffet
ingredients:
  beef meatballs
  pork dumplings
  udon noodles
  savoy cabbage
  pea shoots

43

la catrina

locals only taco truck

9694 southeast 82nd avenue. between lamphier and otty
503.890.5625
mon - sun 9a - 11p

opened in 2007 owner: jose portillo
$: cash
breakfast. lunch. dinner. first come, first served

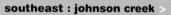

southeast : johnson creek > **e21**

J: Some guidebooks will list any place that serves a drink in a martini glass. Not us. We pride ourselves on leaving no stone unturned. If a place is good and noteworthy, it doesn't matter if the food is served on Royal Copenhagen china or on a napkin that reads, "don't leave your greasy fingerprints behind." *La Catrina* is the latter. This is a taco cart in a gas station parking lot. It's not chic, but it has the best tortas cubanas in town. So be adventurous— you'll find that *La Catrina* is as rewarding (and as delicious) as any fancy-pants joint out there.

imbibe / devour:
jarritos
fresca
tortas cubanas
al pastor taco
huevos con jamon tortas
lengua tacos
quesadillas

le pigeon

frenchy, sexy, fun bistro

738 east burnside. corner of eighth
503.546.8796 www.lepigeon.com
mon - sat 5 - 10p sun 5 - 9p

opened in 2006. owner: paul brady chef: gabriel rucker
$$: all major credit cards accepted
dinner. wine / beer only. reservations recommended

northeast : east burnside >

J: *Le Pigeon* makes me laugh. Though they are certainly serious here, Gabriel and crew seem to have fun even with the eyes of the media watching. Besides Tonya Harding, almost nothing in Portland has received more national attention. The food is cheeky and I don't just mean clever. Beef cheek bourguignon is a complex dish where the cheek is stewed in wine until it is so tender it will fall apart if you say boo. The desserts are an adventure: foie gras profiteroles, cornbread with ice cream and bacon. If it wasn't so good, you might think someone was pulling your leg.

imbibe / devour:
côtes du rhône cairanne rosé
clos de vougeot burgundy
lamb belly, asparagus & pecorino
foot & tail croquette, beans, rosemary & chili
skate, pork belly, orzo & cauliflower
steak, spaetzle, horseradish & stroganoff
beef cheek bourguignon
foie gras profiteroles

little t american baker

light, modern bakery

2600 southeast division street. corner of 26th
503.238.3458 www.littletbaker.com
mon - sat 7a - 5p sun 8a -2p

opened in 2008. owner and chef: tim healea
$: all major credit cards accepted
breakfast. lunch. coffee/tea. first come, first served

southeast : division > **e23**

J: Yes, I watch "Oprah," but I usually don't buy everything she's selling. When she was hocking *The Secret* the you-want-it-just-think-about-it self-help book, my eyes rolled. But today I realized there might be something to that madness. For years I have wished for a modern, airy bakery to open in my neighborhood, and last week *Little T American Baker* did, and it is everything I wished for. Owner Tim was head baker at the venerable *Pearl Bakery* for years, so his cred is golden. Now the crow I will be eating about *The Secret* will be accompanied with a baked currant doughnut and a slice of pecan toast.

imbibe / devour:
foxfire teas & stumptown coffee
coca cola in small bottles
baked currant doughnut
big t granola cookie
pecan toast
pretzel bread
blt on sally lunn bread
meatloaf on baguette

milwaukie popcorn and candyland

sweets heaven

10821 southeast main street. between jackson and monroe (near harrison)
503.654.4846
tue - fri 11a - 5:30p sat 11a - 4p

opened in 1930. owners: pat and kim keehner
$: cash
treats. first come, first served

southeast : old town milwaukie >

K: Here is how I discovered *Milwaukie Popcorn and Candyland*. I was at *Flutter* and I was gazing at (okay, caressing) the most beautifully packaged chocolate truffles. In fact, the whole table was filled with sweet creations all whimsically wrapped in tinsel and hot-pink bows and Liberty of London-esque black-and-white papers. I asked Cindy about the provenance of the treats, and she aimed me to this little heaven on earth for lovers of all things sweet. Outside the door you're in old town Milwaukie (just a stone's throw from Sellwood), inside the door—Paris. Fantastique!

imbibe / devour:
white chocolate popcorn
chocolate dragees
two cases filled with chocolates made in-house
gorgeously packaged truffles
old-fashioned candy buttons
tasty french marshmallows
black licorice beagles

moxie rx

groovy roadside juicebar and trailer café
just north of the intersection of mississippi and shaver (next to fresh pot)
moxierx.blogspot.com
check blogsite for seasonal hours

opened in 2005. owners: nancye benson and william macklin
$ - $$: cash
breakfast. lunch. first come, first served

north : mississippi > **e25**

K: Call the lawyers because I'm stealing "mmm, mmm good" away from Campbell's Soup. Canned chicken noodle soup can't hold a candle to the divine creations that spill forth from Nancye's trailer of goodness called *Moxie RX*. If there's a better place to be on a sunny spring weekend morning in Portland, I haven't found it yet. On the morning I visited, I ordered the sunrise special, which was like eating spring. Perfectly cooked eggs rested on a nest of peppery greens in a vinaigrette and slivers of cured salmon. I'll say it again—mmm, mmm good.

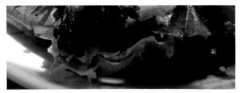

imbibe / devour:
blueberry limeade tonic
mornin' glory remedy
homespun goods baked in the trailer:
  lemon coconut muffin
  blueberry scone
fig & anise panini with goat cheese
sunrise special (greens & eggs)
buckweat belgian waffle

navarre

small plates great glasses

10 northeast 28th avenue. near the corner of burnside
503.232.3555 www.eatnavarre.com
mon - wed 4:30 - 10:30p thu 10:30a - 10:30p fri 10:30a - 11:30p
sat 9:30a - 11:30p sun 9:30a - 10:30p

opened in 2002. owner / chef : john taboada
$$: mc. visa
brunch. lunch. dinner. first come, first served

northeast : east burnside > **e26**

K: I don't have enough spontaneity in my life. There are last minute this and thats—but spontaneity is a different beast. In my handy thesaurus its synonyms are noted as: casualness, easiness, informality, naturalness, poise, unceremoniousness and unrestraint. These all are great descriptors for *Navarre,* where spontaneity creates magic. Here is where you come for food that is cooked passionately but without pretense. For example, chicken on the menu is described as bird. Love it. I don't need the blah blah. I just need good food.

imbibe / devour:
wines they (navarre) choose (three pours)
savoie specials:
  potato & cheese matafan
  croute au abundance
specials
  capon with black trumpets & candied fennel
  pea shoots with breseola
basque cake

nostrana

playing with fire nightly

1401 southeast morrison. corner of 14th
503.234.2427 www.nostrana.com
lunch mon - fri 11:30a - 2p
dinner sun - thu 5 - 10p fri - sat 5 - 11p

opened in 2005. owners: cathy whims and david west chef: cathy whims
$$ - $$$: all major credit cards accepted
lunch. dinner. reservations recommended

southeast : industrial > 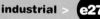 **e27**

K: There's nothing better than Sunday dinner. It's the end of the week, and it feels right to be comforted before plowing into the next week. I suggest a great place to find food solace is *Nostrana*. Their "Sunday in Italy" dinner is four courses, and it's guaranteed to hit all the right spots. If Sunday is your night to be at home still hoping Marlon Perkins's Wild Kingdom will come back on, no worries—any day at *Nostrana* is a good day when the wood-fired oven is kicking out savory, crisp pizzas and the wine is flowing. Your choice—you can't go wrong.

imbibe / devour:
italian 75
99 vietti barolo rocche
shepherd's salad
shiitake & parmigiano fritatta with fiddlehead ferns
housemade potato gnocchi
primavera pizza
bistecca alla fiorentina
wood oven apple & rhubarb crisp

pastaworks

fresh pasta, artisan cheeses and good wine

se / evoe: 3735 southeast hawthorne boulevard. between 37th and 38th. 503.232.1010

city market: 735 northwest 21st avenue. corner of johnson. 503.221.3002

north: 4212 north mississippi avenue. between skidmore and mason

www.pastaworks.com

mon - sat 9:30a - 7p sun 10a - 7p

opened in 1983. owners: the de garmo family

$$: visa. mc

grocery. light meals at evoe. first come, first served

southeast : hawthorne / northwest : nob hill / north : mississippi >

K: I take comfort that in my life there are some things that won't change. I will always have short hair. My dogs will throw themselves against the window when other dogs walk by. And for the nine years since I met my husband Kevin, I knew that his family business *Pastaworks* would always have delicious pasta, cheese and wine at their two locations. But then comes 2008 with change. What? A new location on Mississippi and a new restaurant, *Evoe*, that serves simple sandwiches, savories and wine. What next I wonder? I become a pogo-stick designer? Lola runs off to join the circus? The mysteries of life.

imbibe / devour:
07 abbazia di novacella kerner
handmade garlic whistle saffron ravioli
le poteaupré washed rind cheese
housemade pancetta
warm focaccia
mancianti extra virgin olive oil
paysan breton beurre au sel de mer
strauss family creamery ice cream

pine state biscuits

buttermilk biscuit café

3640 southeast belmont street. between 36th and 37th
503.236.3346 www.pinestatebiscuits.com
tue - sun 7a - 2p

opened in 2008. owners / chefs: kevin atchley, walt alexander and brian snyder
$ - $$: mc. visa
breakfast. lunch. first come, first served

southeast : sunnyside >

J: Living in southeast Portland, I have few complaints. We have some of the best coffee, restaurants and parks in this city. But when *Pine State Biscuits* opened down the street this year, I said fiddle-de-dee... how did we southeasters get so lucky? This is a southern-style biscuit house where all things good come on a freshly made buttermilk biscuit, like gravy and eggs or fried chicken, pickles, mustard and honey. If these taste combos don't make you sing "My Old Kentucky Home," then you must be a Yankee.

imbibe / devour:
cherrywine soda
sweet tea
biscuit sandwiches:
  mcisley
  reggie deluxe
biscuits with shiitake mushroom gravy
the moneyball
cream-topped biscuit with butter & honey

podnah's pit

texas style barbeque

1469 northeast prescott avenue. corner of 15th
503.281.3700 www.podnahspit.com
mon - fri 11a - 9:30p sat - sun 9a - 9:30p

opened in 2006. owner / chef: rodney muirhead owner: kirk kelley
$$: all major credit cards accepted
brunch. lunch. dinner. first come, first served

northeast : king >

K: Portland may be a lot of things, but one thing it's never been, is a great place to eat barbeque. If that's what rings your bell, you're better off heading to Portland's vibracious doppleganger city—Austin. But hold your knickers before you catch a flight because starting in '06, PDX barbeque started looking better with the arrival of *Podnah's Pit*. This is the real stuff, evocative of what you might dig into at the *Salt Lick* or *Kreuz's Market* in Texas, though *Podnah's* is about 800 square feet and those places are about 80,000 square feet. Here in Oregon we do things smaller.

imbibe / devour:
double mountain ipa
iceberg wedge with blue cheese dressing
texas red chili with corn bread
an example bbq plate:
 brisket, pork spare ribs & black-eyed pea salad
pecan pie with cold whoop
finger lickin' good brunch

pok pok / whiskey soda lounge

3226 southeast division. between 32nd and 33rd
503.232.1387 www.pokpokpdx.com
see hours on the website

opened in 2005. owner / chef: andy ricker
$: mc. visa
lunch. dinner. full bar. reservations accepted for parties of five or more at whiskey

southeast : division >

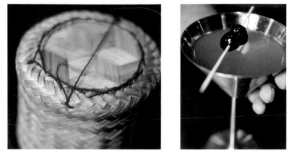

J: You don't expect a Thai restaurant, owned by a white American guy, to be so spectacularly authentic. But *Pok Pok* owner, Andy is not your typical honky. He's traveled to Asia for years, soaking up all the local flavor, and it shows. You can order from a takeout window and sit at the outdoor tables or have more of a restaurant experience at the *Whiskey Soda Lounge*, where you'll find a night-club-meets-Asian-rumpus-room atmosphere. Wherever you plant yourself, once you eat a bite of the grilled game hen spiked with lemongrass, you'll swear you're in Bangkok.

imbibe / devour:
houndstooth cocktail
aviation cocktail
khao man som tam
baa mii pet teun
ike's vietnamese fish sauce wings
kung yak phao
tam kai yaang
coconut ice cream sandwich

portland farmer's market

the best of the country brought to the heart of the city

shemanski park (wed), eastbank (thu), ecotrust (thu) and portland state (sat)
see website for exact addresses, seasonal schedules and hours
503.241.0032 www.portlandfarmersmarket.org

opened in 1992
$ - $$: all major credit cards accepted
first come, first served

different locations >

K: When you see your neighbors driving away on a Saturday morning before 8 a.m., do you wonder what motivates them to rise and shine? A desperate dash for coffee is a good guess, but the truth is that they are probably heading for the *Portland Farmer's Market* at Portland State. This is *the* most festive place in town on a Saturday morning. Parents have children and dogs in tow and coffee in hand all while perusing the most verdant produce, the freshest of cheeses, and scads of other delicacies all from local farmers and food purveyors. This place is a cornucopia of deliciousness.

imbibe / devour:
some favorites:
  alma chocolate
  viridian farms
  café velo
  cherry country
  fressen bakery
  willamette valley cheese co.
  sol pops

random order coffeehouse & bakery

save room for pie

1800 northeast alberta avenue. corner of 18th
503.331.1420 www.randomordercoffee.com
daily 6:30a - 11p

opened in 2004. owner: tracy olson baker: kate mcmillan
$: all major credit cards accepted
breakfast. light meals. coffee / tea. treats. first come, first served

northeast : alberta > **e33**

K: Sometimes I get bored with breakfast. I don't want to, because I love breakfast whole-bodily. And so, when I'm feeling a tinge of early morn ennui, I know what the answer is and where to get it: pie at *Random Order*. Pie is the perfect breakfast, and this shouldn't be disputed. It goes well with both coffee and tea, it's filled with fruit and therefore healthy, and the crust is a carb wonderland, so you don't feel hungry five minutes after eating. See—pie is the ultimate food. And the ones that Kate makes here are dee-vine. I recently had a berry/rhubarb slice for breakfast, and hot damn—it made my day.

imbibe / devour:
iced toddy coffee
sangria & sunday bloody sunday
world famous fried egg sandwich
velvet elvis panini
don rickles sandwich
rhubarb cardamom pie
flirty berry pie
banana cream pie

red coach restaurant

old-school downtown lunch spot

615 southwest broadway avenue. between alder and morrison
503.227.4840
mon - fri 11a - 3p

opened in 1963. owners: bob and jeanne durkheimer
$ - $$: cash
lunch. first come, first served

southwest : downtown > 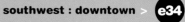 **e34**

J: *Red Coach Restaurant* is an old school, hidden sliver of a restaurant that seems to have forgotten to turn the calendar for a few years. Here, people eat burgers and fries every day, salads exist mostly for the ladies, and credit cards don't exist. Lined with red-tufted vinyl booths and filling a space between two office buildings, *Red Coach's* wedge of a location doesn't seem to be going anywhere. And why should it? Waiters know everyone's names, and the food is very good and efficiently served. Secret places that evoke simpler times will always be in style.

imbibe / devour:
chocolate milkshake
cherry coke
chili plate
sloppy joe
dinner salad with tuna & cheese
karl's special cheeseburger
blt
tuna melt with fries

sahagún

exquisite handmade chocolates

10 northwest 16th avenue. between burnside and couch
503.274.7065 www.sahagunchocolates.com
wed - sat 10am - 6pm   closed during the month of august

opened in 2005. owner / chef: elizabeth montes
$: mc. visa
coffee / hot chocolate. treats. first come, first served

northwest : lower nob hill > **e35**

K: Sometimes when I walk through a park with Lola, we stop to watch the little kids gathered around a muddy patch, intently concocting "all-natural" creations that they then offer their parents to eat because it is, after-all, a luscious mud chiffon pie. I imagine that Elizabeth as a child created some pretty extraordinary mud treats, and those early recipes have now turned into the delightful and absolutely edible chocolate wonders at her tiny cacao palace, *Sahagún*. Here Elizabeth's whimsical aesthetic meets up with chocolate-making mastery and the results are total bliss.

imbibe / devour:
chile limon b-side soda
beyond divine hot chocolate
figalicious
crackle pops!
oregon kiss
rose geranium
marzipan drops
homemade ice cream

steve's cheese

going to great lengths for stellar cheese
2321 northwest thurman street (inside square deal wine company)
between 23rd place and 23rd avenue
503.222.6014 www.stevescheese.biz
tue - sat 11a -7p sun - mon noon - 6p

opened in 2006. owner: steve jones
$ - $$: all major credit cards accepted
grocery. classes and events. first come, first served

northwest : nob hill >

K: Cheese lovers are a loyal breed, and once they have bonded with a cheesemaster, they've bonded for life. I know many who are devout followers of Steve. And he's made it easy to find him by naming his cool little nook inside of *Square Deal Wine Co.*, *Steve's Cheese*. Smart man, good cheese. He doesn't have a lot of space here, so he features just his favorites and they are all well vetted. The day I was in, I sampled the Cowgirl Creamery cottage cheese. Who knew that cottage cheese could be so luscious? I could have eaten a bucket full. I now am a follower of Steve also.

imbibe / devour:
neal's yard berkswell
cowgirl creamery cottage cheese
sottocenere al tartufo
assorted charcuterie
deux chas pumpkin ginger focaccia crackers
ames farm single source honey
nonna's noodles
square deal wines

stumptown annex

coffee beans and tasting room

3352 southeast belmont street. between 33rd and 34th

503.467.4123 www.stumptowncoffee.com

mon - sun 8a - 8p

opened in 2005. owner : duane sorenson

$ - $$: mc. visa

coffee. first come, first served

southeast : sunnyside >

J: Portland is a city of rock stars. There are the hyper-cool indie kids playing their catchy, jangly tunes, and a handful of older musicians who have come here to pasture. Even our local coffee purveyor has national rock-star status. *Stumptown Coffee* is the "it" coffee at cafés in cities nationwide. And rather than sit on their cool laurels, they are doing something classy by educating people about how to taste and appreciate the roasted bean. At the handsome *Stumptown Annex*, there are twice-daily "cuppings" where the learning happens. *Stumptown*, you are already legendary.

imbibe / devour:
stumptown coffee:
  ethiopia tega & tula
  yemen sharasi
  rwanda musasa horizon
  nicaragua los delirios el cipres
  honduras cielito lindo
  costa rica el quemado
  bolivia san ignacio

tanuki

sake no sakana (food that goes with sake)

413 northwest 21st avenue. between glisan and flanders
503.241.7667 www.tanukipdx.com
tue - thu noon - 9p fri - sat noon - 10p

opened in 2008. owner / chef: janis martin
$$: mc. visa
lunch. dinner. first come, first served

northwest : nob hill > **e38**

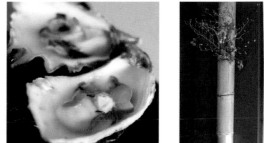

K: I apologize. I realize that most of you perusing this guide may not read Japanese, and therefore have no idea what I have listed below under devour. So my suggestion is to embrace the photos—they are worth a thousand words—and more importlandly, visit *Tanuki*. Soon. This welcoming little spot is fashioned after what the Japanese call an "izakaya" or a drinking establishment that serves food. At *Tanuki* you'll find artfully presented little plates of food that embody the flavors of Japan while drawing upon northwest bounty, sometimes grown in Janis's garden. Delicious.

imbibe / devour:
japanese drinking vinegars
wakame to shiitake su
tamago-hotate
hotate han-aki no kakune
o-maguro shiro
ton-tsukune
soba in a rich duck broth with egg

tastebud

wood-fired rustic baking and food

3220 southeast milwaukie. just south of powell
503.234.0330 www.tastebudfarm.com
wed - sat 5 - 10p

opened in 2008. owner / chef: mark doxtader
$$: all major credit cards accepted
dinner. catering / private events. first come, first served

southeast : brooklyn >

K: The first time I met Mark was at the Portland Farmer's Market. I stood transfixed—watching this fir tree of a man as he stoked the fire of his mobile wood-fired brick oven. Out of that oven came glorious breads and perfectly grilled meats and veggies, which he pieced together to make freakin' amazing sandwiches. Since that time I have eaten Mark's food on many occasions, and when I heard that he was opening a restaurant, I shed a happy tear. This is somebody who has *the* touch, and his simple, rustic creations are pure bliss and evocative of what Portland is all about.

imbibe / devour:
villa di carlo dolce lambrusco
montreal style bagels
pizza:
   dandelion marmalade of greens, olives,
     capers & currants
   chilies & anchovies
   lamb sausage, ricotta & arugula
cheese cake with rhubarb jam

the country cat

dinnerhouse and bar

7937 southeast stark. corner of 80th
503.408.1414 www.thecountrycat.net
brunch sat - sun 9a - 2p
dinner daily 5p - close

opened in 2007. owners: adam and jackie sappington. chef: adam sappington
$$: all major credit cards accepted
brunch. dinner. reservations accepted for parties of four or more

southeast : montavilla > 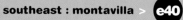 **e40**

K: Recently Lola, my daughter, announced she was a vegetarian. Her last meal before the big declaration began with bacon-wrapped shrimp and grits at *The Country Cat*. She licked the plate clean. Kevin and I knew vegetarianism would be short-lived for our pork-centric child. I, too, am a lover of the pig, but could also be a "friedchickenetarian." And the *Cat* is where my people come to worship. Behold the picture at left and bow down. God bless the bird in its fried glory, and praise be to Adam who is the one who cooks it.

imbibe / devour:
kentucky housewife
cold bud
fried shrimp cocktail
bacon-wrapped white gulf shrimp
crispy fried snow crab hush puppies
cast-iron skillet fried chicken
pan-roasted arctic char
butterscotch pudding

the meadow

the elements of good living

3731 north mississippi avenue. corner of beach
503.288.4633 www.atthemeadow.com
sun - tue 11a - 6p wed - sat 11a - 7p

opened in 2006. owners: mark and jennifer bitterman
$$ - $$$: all major credit cards accepted
first come, first served

north : mississippi > **e41**

J: Salt is the new, well... salt. Yes, there are food trends, just like in fashion. Remember truffle powder and bee pollen? Not to be dismissive—trends mark a moment and that's great, but I'm always happy when a classic like salt comes back into vogue. Not Morton's, mind you, but the exotic stuff. To become freshly acquainted with this old friend, you need to visit *The Meadow*, where they carry a vast selection and are most happy to educate. And if you feel a friendship with chocolate is important, you'll find many new friends here co-mingling with the salt and other good-living imperatives.

imbibe / devour:
starter salt sets
house-salted chocolates
himalayan salt plates
fee brothers artisanal bitters
vya dry vermouth
pineau des charentes pineau
amedei chocolates
peugeot pepper mills

toast

a great neighborhood restaurant

5222 southeast 52nd avenue. corner of steele
503.774.1020 www.toastwoodstock.com
wed - sun 8a - 2p for dinner hours see website

opened in 2007. owner: donald kotler
$$: mc. visa
brunch. dinner. first come, first served

southeast : woodstock > **e42**

K: Some of the names of the dishes at *Toast* are pretty amusing. I apologize I don't have the space here to tell you them all, so I'm just going to focus on my favorite: Take the Leap. And so I did—I dived into pork belly before noon nirvana. Look and drool at the picture to your left. Is that the most beautiful slab of pork you've ever seen? And when it's draped on top of a potato rosti and two over-easy eggs, it's a monumentally spectacular dish of decadence. Pile it all on a piece of the housemade toast, and yo' tummy will be humming happy songs.

imbibe / devour:
courier coffee
toast's bloody mary
bad ass breakfast sandwich
take the leap
fregola sardo
the new stop p.m.
homemade breads (toast!) & english muffins
apple chiffon cake

toro bravo

incredible spanish tapas

120 northeast russell street. between rodney and mlk
503.281.4464 www.torobravopdx.com
sun - thu 5 - 10p fri - sat 5 - 11p

opened in 2007. owners: john gorham and courtney wilson-gorham chef: john gorham
$$: all major credit cards accepted
dinner. full bar
reservations accepted for parties of seven or more only between sun - thu

northeast : mlk >

J: If someone offered you fifty bucks or immediate seating at *Toro Bravo*, what would you do? Take the table! The fantastic tapas at this year-old sensation are definitely a prize. The large menu of tapas are consistently awesome and are best when shared by a table of friends. And the perpetually full dining room is always buzzy, fueled by delicious cocktails and housemade sangria. It all adds up to a recipe for fun, one that might inspire an "olé!" or two by the end of the night.

imbibe / devour:
casa rita
house sangria
sherry chicken liver mousse
tortilla with nettles
spicy octopus, calamari & prawn stew
sautéed kale with sunny side up egg
smoked pork with grilled bread & celery root
boquerones on toast with pipérade

two tarts bakery

artisan sweets for the soul

2309 northwest kearney avenue. corner of 23rd
503.910.6694 www.twotartsbakery.com
tue - sun 11a - 6p

opened in 2008. owners: elizabeth beekley and anna phelps baker: elizabeth beekley
$: all major credit cards accepted
treats. catering. first come, first served

northwest : nob hill > 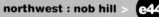 **e44**

K: Every year when the Girl Scouts start to sell cookies I get excited. Not normal excited, but slightly deranged excited. I got this same feeling when I heard that the *Two Tarts Bakery* gals were opening up a storefront. I felt like rushing to the nearest mountaintop and twirling like Julie Andrews in *The Sound of Music*. Instead I decided to contact them directly to see if I had heard correctly. I had. Yay and another twirl. *Two Tarts* cookies are sweet joy in a little package. It's hard to choose which is my favorite, so I'll just say I love them all, and so will you.

imbibe / devour:
french-pressed coffee
double-chocolate chews
anzac biscuits
pecan tessies
cappuccino creams
peanut butter creams
hazelnut baci

ya hala

lebanese cuisine

8005 southeast stark street. corner of 80th
503.256.4484 www.yahalrestaurant.com
mon - sat 11a - 9p

opened in 1999. owner: john attar. owner / chef: mirna attar
$$: all major credit cards accepted
lunch. dinner. full bar. first come, first served

southeast : montavilla >

J: I sometimes like to imagine what the "American Idol" judges would say if they were at a restaurant with me trying the food. At *Ya Hala*, I think they would sound something like this. Randy: "Yo, dog. Listen up. I have always said if you can cook, you can cook anything, and you can cook it well." Paula would give an addled hug of a compliment like, "The kanafe makes me want to cry it's so good." And Simon (on a nice day) would say, "The fasoulia is consistently incredible, but your falafel is the best I've ever had. Get ready to be a star." And in this rare instance, I would have to agree with Simon.

imbibe / devour:
rose water soda
guava drop
fasoulia
makloube
lamb shank with saffron cream
arnabeet
katayef
kanafe

• all of the businesses featured in this book are locally owned. in deciding the businesses to feature, we require this first and foremost. and then we look for businesses that strike us as utterly authentic, whether they be new or old, chic or funky. and since this is not an advertorial guide, businesses do not pay to be featured.

• explore from neighborhood to neighborhood. note that almost every neighborhood featured has dozens of great stores and restaurants other than our favorites listed in this book.

• the maps in this guide are not highly detailed but instead are representational of each area noted. we highly suggest, if you are visiting, to also have a more detailed map. streetwise maps are always a good bet, and are easy to fold up and take along with you.

• make sure to double check the hours of the business before you go by calling or visiting its website. often the businesses change their hours seasonally. also, businesses that are featured sometimes close. this is often the sobering reality for many small, local businesses.

• the pictures and descriptions of each business are representational. please don't be distraught when the business no longer carries or is not serving something you saw or read about in the guide.

• the *eat.shop* clan consists of a small crew of creative types who travel extensively and have dedicated themselves to great eating and interesting shopping around the world. each of these people writes, photographs and researches his or her own books. in this case, two people shared the duties. so there are two voices at play, which are noted as either "k" (kaie) or "j" (jon).

• there are three ranges of prices noted for restaurants, $ = cheap, $$ = medium, $$$ = expensive

• if you own the previous editions of *eat.shop portland*, make sure to keep them. think of the each edition as part of an overall "volume" of books, as many of the businesses no longer featured are still open and still fantastic. and note, the reason businesses are no longer featured in the guide is not because we don't like them anymore, but because there are so many amazing businesses that need a chance to be featured. to see past businesses, go to our website where all editions are available in online or e-book format.

eat.shop.sleep

there are many great places to stay in portland, but here are a few of our picks:

the ace hotel
1022 sw stark street (west end)
503.228.2277 / acehotel.com
standard double with shared bath $90
delux double with private bath $140
restaurants: clyde common, stumptown coffee
notes: chic utilatarian

hotel modera
515 sw clay street (downtown : near portland state)
503.484.1084 / hotelmodera.com
standard double from $145
notes: modern and affordable

hotel delux
729 sw fifth avenue (downtown : near civic stadium)
503.219.2094 / hoteldeluxeportland.com
standard double from $190
restaurants: gracie's
bar: the driftwood room
notes: glam, old hollywood

the benson
309 southwest broadway (downtown)
503.228.2000 / bensonhotel.com
standard double from $190
restaurant: the london grill
notes: old portland landmark

the jupiter hotel
800 east burnside street (east burnside)
503.230.9200 / jupiterhotel.com
standard double from $125
restaurant and club: doug fir
notes: live music and lodging

- **sellwood**
  - **west-moreland**

eat

e18 > garden state
e24 > milwaukie popcorn and candyland

shop

s15 > gr scrubb
s24 > madison park
s32 > spielwerk
s34 > ste. maine
s37 > tilde
s40 > why not?

oaks pioneer park

se 14th
s34
se bybee blvd
se rural st
se ogden st
se milwaukie ave
se knapp st
se flavel st
se rex st
se malden st
se lambert st
s24
se bidwell st
e18
se lexington st
s37
se miller st
s32
se nehalem st
se 7th
se 11th
se 13th
se 15th
se 16th
se tacoma st
se tenino st
s15
se umatilla st
s40
se 17th ave
e24

note: all maps face north

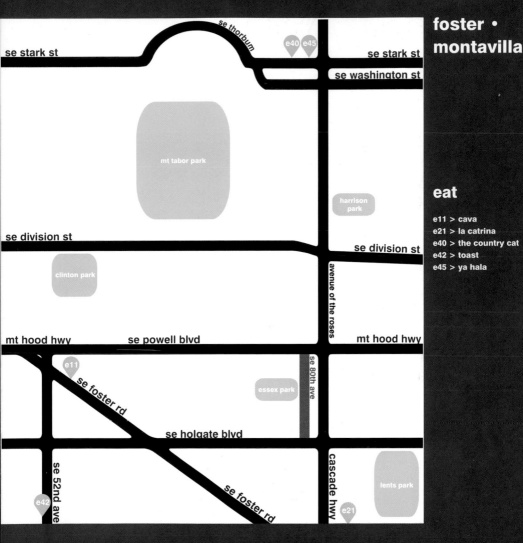

foster •
montavilla

se thorbum

se stark st
e40 e45
se stark st

se washington st

mt tabor park

harrison
park

eat

e11 > cava
e21 > la catrina
e40 > the country cat
e42 > toast
e45 > ya hala

se division st
se division st

clinton park

avenue of the roses

mt hood hwy
se powell blvd
mt hood hwy

se 80th ave

e11
se foster rd

essex park

se holgate blvd

se 52nd ave

cascade hwy

lents park

se foster rd

e42
e21

note: all maps face north

- **brooklyn**
- **clinton**
- **division**
- **hawthorne**
- **sunnyside (belmont)**

eat

e6 > belmont station
e9 > broder
e10 > castagna
e23 > little t american baker
e27 > nostrana
e28 > pastaworks
e29 > pine state biscuits
e31 > pok pok whiskey soda lounge
e37 > stumptown annex
e39 > tastebud

shop

s3 > beckel canvas
s10 > elsa + sam
s14 > green noise
s19 > langlitz leather
s22 > local 35
s23 > look modern
s36 > the perfume house
s41 > xtabay

se morrison st
se belmont st
se belmont st
se hawthorne blvd
se 35th av
se 34th ave
se 20th ave
se 12th ave
se 11th ave
division st
se division st
se clinton st
se tibbetts st
se powell blvd
mt hood hwy
se milwaukie ave
powell park
se 26th ave

note: all maps face north

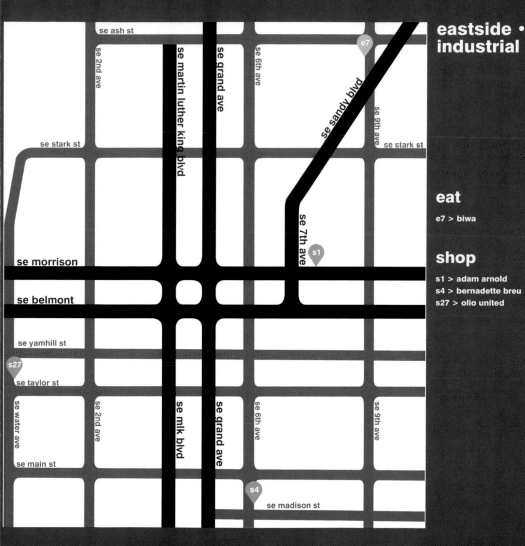

eastside •
industrial

eat

e7 > biwa

shop

s1 > adam arnold
s4 > bernadette breu
s27 > olio united

note: all maps face north

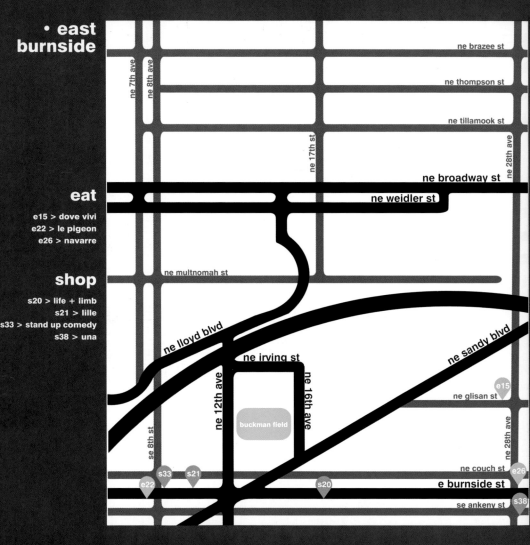

• **east burnside**

eat

e15 > dove vivi
e22 > le pigeon
e26 > navarre

shop

s20 > life + limb
s21 > lille
s33 > stand up comedy
s38 > una

ne brazee st
ne thompson st
ne tillamook st
ne broadway st
ne weidler st
ne multnomah st
ne lloyd blvd
ne irving st
ne sandy blvd
ne glisan st
ne couch st
e burnside st
se ankeny st

ne 7th ave
ne 8th ave
ne 17th st
ne 28th ave
ne 12th ave
ne 16th ave
se 8th st
ne 28th ave

buckman field

e15
e26
e22
s33
s21
s20
s38

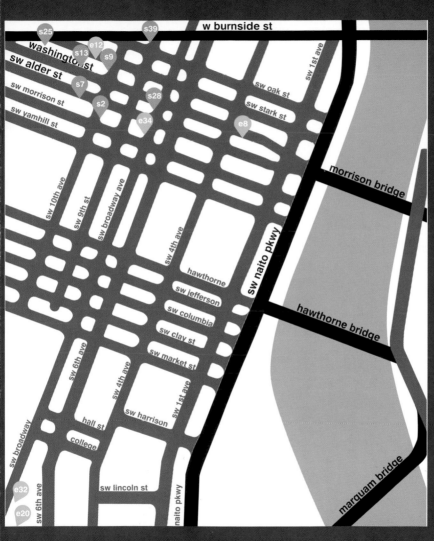

downtown •
west end •

eat

e2 > alba osteria
e8 > blueplate
e12 > clyde common
e20 > hot pot city
e32 > portland
farmer's market
e34 > red coach

shop

s2 > am-living
s7 > canoe
s9 > covet
s13 > frances may
s25 > odessa
s28 > pinkham millinery
s39 > velo shop

note: all maps face north

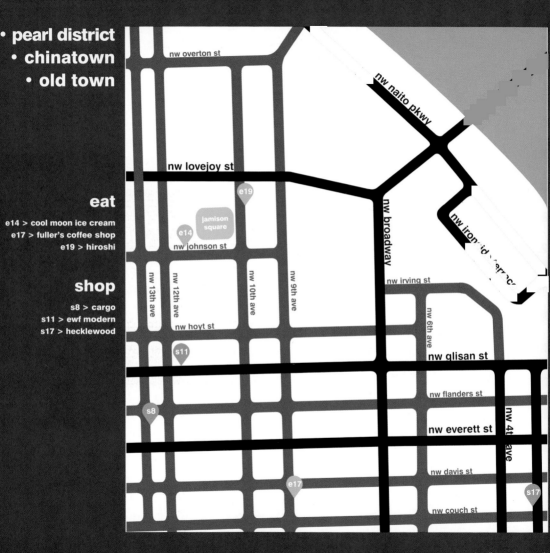

- **pearl district**
- **chinatown**
- **old town**

eat

e14 > cool moon ice cream
e17 > fuller's coffee shop
e19 > hiroshi

shop

s8 > cargo
s11 > ewf modern
s17 > hecklewood

nw overton st

nw naito pkwy

nw lovejoy st

e19

jamison square

e14

nw johnson st

nw broadway

nw iron...

nw 13th ave

nw 12th ave

nw 10th ave

nw 9th ave

nw irving st

nw hoyt st

nw 6th ave

s11

nw glisan st

nw flanders st

s8

nw everett st

nw 4th ave

nw davis st

e17

s17

nw couch st

note: all maps face north

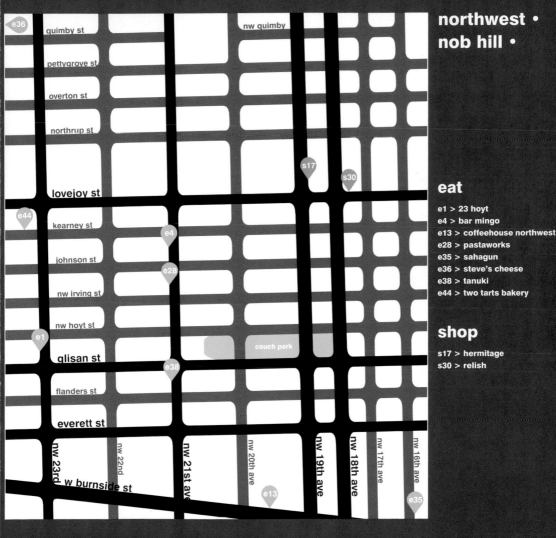

northwest •
nob hill •

eat

e1 > 23 hoyt
e4 > bar mingo
e13 > coffeehouse northwest
e28 > pastaworks
e35 > sahagun
e36 > steve's cheese
e38 > tanuki
e44 > two tarts bakery

shop

s17 > hermitage
s30 > relish

note: all maps face north

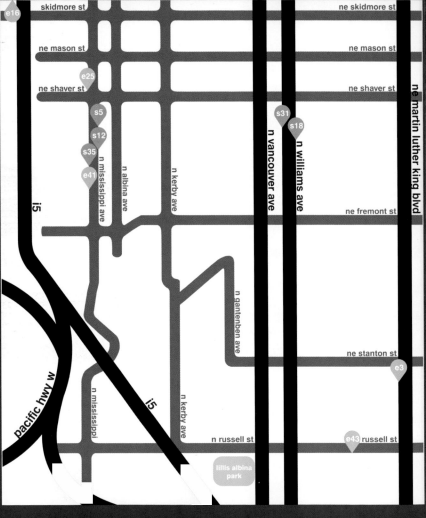

mississippi
- williams
- mlk

eat

e3 > alu
e16 > flavourspot
e25 > moxie rx
e41 > the meadow
e43 > toro bravo

shop

s5 > black wagon
s12 > flutter
s18 > ink & peat
s31 > scrap
s35 > sunlan

note: all maps face north

concordia •
beaumont •
wilshire
king •

eat

e5 > beast
e30 > podnah's
e33 > random order
coffeehouse

shop

s6 > camellia pure beauty
s26 > office
s29 > popina

note: all maps face north

adam arnold

727 southeast morrison street. between seventh and eighth
503.234.1376 www.adam-arnold.com
by appointment only

opened in 2003. owner: adam arnold
cash only
custom orders

southeast : industrial > s01

J: I know that we can't all be artists making stuff for a living. Some of us have to save the economy, repair the roads and write the guidebooks. So thank God there are people like *Adam Arnold*—his life is a commitment to creativity. This bike-riding student of Esperanto has chosen a path less traveled in order to follow his bliss of hand-making spotlessly tailored clothes for men and women. And though I certainly appreciate a well engineered bridge as I drive across one, I may applaud more the ability to bring joy to people by making them look beautiful. A good life, indeed.

covet:
women's:
  laser dress
  pleated yolk shorts
  chevron dress
men's
  custom shirts
  pleated jeans
  pucker pocket jacket

am-living

where everything tells a story
600 southwest tenth avenue, suite 114. corner of morrison
1.866.700.9200 www.am-living.com
mon - fri 10a - 7p sat 10a - 6p sun 11a - 5p

opened in 2007. owner: haring piebenga
all major credit cards accepted
online shopping

southwest : downtown > 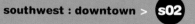 **s02**

K: The first time that *AM-Living* came on my radar was when I stumbled onto a blog where the person was talking about the "cool boat model place downtown." Huh? I'm a native, and I was racking my brain trying to figure out what blog-boy was talking about. Then as I was driving up Morrison, behold! There, taking up the whole southwest corner of The Galleria was *AM-Living* filled with reproductions of boats and planes and zeppelins and balloons. I couldn't park fast enough. Walking in here feels like being on the set of *Around the World in 80 Days*.

covet:
am-living collection:
   vintage helium balloon models
   the entire collection of boat & plane models
   sailor's valentine
   lion weather vane
   antique globes
   the eye of time
   pirate ship kit

beckel canvas products

handmade tents and bags
2232 southeast clinton street. corner of 23rd
800.237.3362 / 503.232.3362 www.beckelcanvas.com
mon - fri 8a - 5p sat 9a - noon

opened in 1964. owner: kathy darnielle
mc. visa
custom orders

southeast : clinton > **s03**

J: Printed on every *Beckel Canvas* product is the Chinook word "eena." This translates to "the beaver who makes the best lodge." *Beckel* has been making the best old-style wall tents for over 40 years. If you don't need a tent, this enterprising company also makes really excellent canvas bags and totes all behind their unassuming little storefront. The place has a Yosemite Sam, gold-panning feel about it, with yards of natural-colored canvas billowed out on large worktables, waiting for a tailor to make it into something great. Leave it to eena.

covet:
beckel canvas:
  roundabout bag
  possibilities bag
  canvas briefcase
  handitote bag
  war bag
  camping pads
  tote bag

bernadette breu

heirloom-quality antiques
1338 southeast sixth avenue. corner of madison
503.226.6565 www.bernadettebreuantiques.com
thu - sat 11a - 6p sun noon - 5p mon 11a - 6p

opened in 2007. owner: bernadette breu
mc. visa
registries. design services

southeast : industrial > **s04**

J: Watching the "Antiques Roadshow" is fun. On the show, guests show their items to a panel of experts—and soon they learn that they own a national treasure and it's worth a fortune. Tears ensue. If you don't think you own such treasures but want to find some—*Bernadette Breu* is filled with them waiting to be discovered. In her new location, a large open warehouse displays her unique collection of objects, furniture, rugs, art and oddities. Though there's no guarantee of potential windfall, the odds are pretty good you'll find something you think is a gem.

covet:
antique mercury lamp
french marble café tables
concrete frog sculpture
taxidermy birds & big-game heads
silver trays with domes
antler chandelier
antique world globes
pink tufted velvet carved frame chair

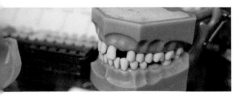

black wagon

groovy style for cool kids

3964 north mississippi avenue. between shaver and failing
503.916.0000 866.916.0004 (toll free) www.blackwagon.com
mon - fri 11a - 7p sat 10a - 7p sun 10a - 5p

opened in 2006. owner: sarah s. shaoul
mc. visa
online shopping. special orders. personal shopping

north : mississippi > 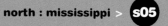 **s05**

K: My daughter Lola is seven. Soon she'll be eight, and then—gasp, nine. Watching her grow up quickly is emotional, but what really makes me verklempt is knowing that soon she won't be able to fit into *Black Wagon's* amazing kids' clothing. Hold please, while I wipe away a tear. Sarah has done the most amazing job of stocking cool kids clothes and accessories that parents love and kids really want to wear. Lola thinks that clothes from here are the bomb and is planning soon to picket to get *Black Wagon* to order sizes nine and up... listening, Sarah?

covet:
egg + avocado everything!
french bull melamine plateware
sand cassel cherry pop cap
lucky fish t's
matthew porter board books
zid zid handmade babuches
super natural baby bedding
vans!

camellia pure beauty

all-natural and organic treats for body, skin and hair

4941 northeast fremont. at 50th
503.287.4645 www.camelliapurebeauty.com
see website for hours

opened in 2007. owner: emily headen
mc. visa
online shopping

northeast : beaumont / wilshire >

K: On a daily basis there are many things to worry about: Will global warming make it snow in July? Have I poisoned myself after drinking the milk that's been in the fridge for a month? And how do I solve the problem of dry cuticles? Some of these things are out of my control, but I know I can head over to the charming and soothing *Camellia Pure Beauty* and get a fantastic salve for the dry cuticle problem. And while there, I can pick up any manner of fantastic all-natural beauty products that will make me feel better through all the worry that life might throw my way.

covet:
kimberly sayer skincare
deep steep moisture sticks
beecrowbee products
shebas secrets bath bomb
nvey organic cosmetics
primitive natural skin care
little twig kids skincare
chidoriya silk & rice bran soap

117

canoe

beautiful gifts and objects

1136 southwest alder street. corner of 12th
503.889.8545 www.canoeonline.net
tue - sat 10a - 6p sun noon - 5p

opened in 2005. owners: craig olson and sean igo
mc. visa
online shopping. registries. special orders

downtown : west end > **s07**

J: It seems there is always a birthday, wedding or housewarming that requires a gift. All of which demand something unique and thoughtful—it can get overwhelming. Here's your answer: *Canoe*. Everything in this beautifully designed shop is covetable and giftable. For example, the pelican-shaped bottle opener is always a hit and says, "I am so excited that you are 37!" Or, "Thank you for hiring me for that freelance job, have this Heath ceramic vase." You are guaranteed to be rehired. And best of all, the nice *Canoe* folks will wrap your purchases so you're good to go.

covet:
heath ceramics
filson bags
aalto savoy vase
lynn read blown-glass vases
stelton stainless teapot
noguchi akari lights
great architecture & design books
pendleton national park blankets

119

cargo

colorful universe of antiques, new furniture and artifacts from asia

380 northwest 13th avenue. between everett and flanders
503.239.8349 www.cargoinc.com
daily 11a - 6p

opened in 1995. owners: patty merrill and brigid blackburn
all major credit cards accepted
online shopping

northwest : pearl district > 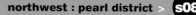 **s08**

K: When you read about Portland in the national press, they always note these places as must-see destinations: Powell's (duh), the Rose Gardens (hello—not the basketball arena, the actual gardens at Washington Park). You get the idea. But I must add that *Cargo* is truly a tourist destination as it's a colorful world of its own, and the size of a small South American country. Here you'll find a vibrant array of goodies from Asia and other parts of the world that will make your head spin. Swooning is not an option, but buying is.

covet:
tibetan recycled plastic bowls
asian antique & reproduction furniture as far
  as the eye can see
'70s chinese propaganda posters
vast collection of plastic grasses
books, books, books
colorful chinese paper decorations
matisse - the clothing store within cargo

covet

429 southwest tenth avenue. between stark and washington
503.222.6838 www.lovecovet.com
mon - sat 11a - 7p sun noon - 5p

opened in 2008. owner: athena frazier
all major credit cards accepted

southwest : west end > 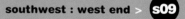 **s09**

K: Weekday mornings when my daughter exists somewhere between consciousness and deep sleep (closer to the latter), I ask her if she wants me to choose some clothes for her. The answer is usually a grunt signifying yes. And this makes me think that I wouldn't mind somebody doing this for me. My husband? Please. I would chose Athena because she understands the importance of classic clothing that's easy to wear yet has a personality. Her lovely new boutique *Covet* is filled with these pieces and yes—she'll be there to guide you to great choices.

covet:
geren ford
tibi
citizens of humanity
chaiken profile
pathway
calleen cordero
wasabi jewelry
dogeared jewelry

elsa + sam

a dishware boutique
4314 southeast hawthorne boulevard. corner of 43rd
503.517.9942 www.elsasam.com
tue - sat 11a - 6p

opened in 2008. owner: elsa edens
all major credit cards accepted
online shopping. registries. custom orders/design

southeast : hawthorne > 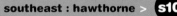 s10

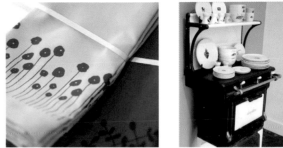

K: Though I love Greek food, I tend to veer away from a certain type of Greek restaurant—specifically the ones where they throw plates. Why are the Greeks hostile toward porcelain? Personally, I can't stand to see a good plate shattered. I would be doubly depressed if I owned some of the pretty dishware, glassware or ceramics from *Elsa + Sam* and I fumbled any of them to oblivion. You won't find the run-of-the-mill white dishware here, but candy-colored, groovily illustrated ceramics that are sourced mainly from independent designers and craftpeople from Brooklyn to Berlin. Delicious.

covet:
kühn keramik ceramics
circa ceramics
michelle brusegaard linens
giarimi design crystal
12fifteen coasters & cards
anna kraitz porcelain
ola design coasters
april stephens dish art

125

ewf modern

environmentally friendly, modern furniture and accessories

1122 northwest glisan. between 11th and 12th
503.295.7336 www.ewfmodern.com
mon - sat 11a - 6p sun noon - 5p

opened in 2007. owner: renee russo
all major credit cards accepted
custom orders / design. hospitality services

northwest : pearl district > 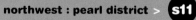 **s11**

K: Living here in Oregon, you take trees for granted. They are everywhere around us and a part of our mythology. When east coasters are asked what comes to mind when asked about Oregon, they note, "rain. trees. beer." Fair enough. So it's apropos that *EWF Modern* features a whole array of furniture (dining, living and bedroom) that is created out of re-claimed hardwood and sustainably harvested wood. It's all quite modern, yet at the same time warm and comforting (and comfortable!). Mix these pieces with chic white and stainless accessories, and it's a formula for highly desirable.

covet:
ewf modern:
  organic collection
  brazil collection
nicoletti leather sofa
white ceramics:
  kavi pradeep thangaraj
  klein reid
exotic cowhide rugs

flutter

a delightful disarray of found objects and clutter

3948 north mississippi avenue. between shaver and failing
503.288.1649 www.flutterclutter.com
mon - wed 11a - 6p thu - sat 11a - 8p sun 11a - 5p

opened in 2006. owner: cindy rokoff
all major credit cards accepted
online shopping

north : mississippi > 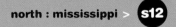 **s12**

K: When I look at the list of covets below, it looks lean. *Flutter* is the type of place where just having eight spaces to note the things I really want is absolutely not enough. From the moment I step through the door here, my eye can identify at least a dozen objects that are im-per-a-tive to my ongoing happiness. As I explore further, I'm looking around to see if there are any full-size shopping carts as there's such a plethora of the right stuff, including the Frocky Jack Morgan "store-within-a-store." If I embrace the steampunk style, Frocky will be my outfitter of choice.

covet:
flutter bedding
frocky jack morgan
red sconces
crazylibellule's shanghaijava perfumes
large & small mandibles
musical birdcages (and also real birdcages!)
pixie stix!

frances may

sentimental women's clothing

1013 southwest washington. between 10th and 11th
503.227.3402 www.francesmay.net
mon - sat 11a - 7p sun noon - 6p

opened in 2008. owner: pamela baker-miller
all major credit cards accepted

southwest : west end > 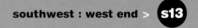 **s13**

K: When I was a child growing up here in Portland, my mother, grandmother and I would, on special days, get dressed in our finery and head downtown for a day of shopping at *I. Magnin* and *Meier & Frank*. These memories are etched into me. When Pamela shared with me that her co-buyer at *Frances May* is her grandmother, I immediately connected with her and that bond between generations, and how it informs the carefully chosen, beautifully crafted clothing in this fetching store that seems at once modern, and yet sentimental. Here's to all the women who make us who we are today.

covet:
church + state
rachel comey
samantha pleet
laura seymour
lorick
ernest sewn
thea grant jewelry
emily baker jewelry

green noise records

punk, hardcore and indie music store
2615 southeast clinton street. between 26th and 27th
503.736.0909 www.greennoiserecords.com
mon - sat noon - 8p sun noon - 5p

opened in 2005. owner: ken cheppaikode
mc. visa
online shopping. custom orders

southeast : clinton > 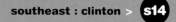 **s14**

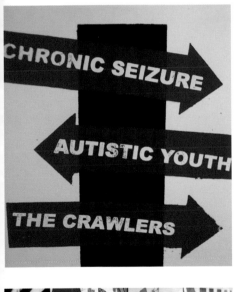

J: This city is full of awesome record stores. So how do you go about choosing a favorite? If you're after the soundtrack from *Titanic*, you are probably fine going to the music department at Freddy's. But if your taste leans more to punk and hardcore—*Green Noise* is as strong as it gets. Ken's selection and knowledge of these genres is unsurpassed. Also, as the the owner of Dirtnap Records, he can offer a unique perspective without a whiff of rock-and-roll snobbery. But unfortunately, he might not be able to help you with acquiring Ms. Dion.

covet:
new & used:
  vinyl
  cds
  cassettes
  45s
  rock dvds
comic mags & zines
rock t's

gr scrub

all manner of materials and tools for a clean house

8235 southeast 13th avenue #12. between tenino and umatilla
503.236.8986 www.grscrub.com
tue - sat 11a - 5p

opened in 2006. owner: glenn recchia
mc. visa
online shopping

southeast : sellwood > 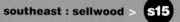 **s15**

K: I would love to tell you that since I first met Glenn and fell in love with *GR Scrub*, that my home has become a cleaner place. It hasn't. But this is not a reflection on Glenn or the amazing products he carries. All blame goes on dirt. Who created this dirt stuff anyway? It's a real pain, and no matter what I do, it won't go away. I guess if I didn't have one husband, one kid, two dogs, one cat and one hamster (and let's not forget the naughty house mice), maybe the dirt would disappear. In the meantime, I will continue to purchase all I need in my war against dirt at *GR Scrub*. Huzzah!

covet:
ulster weavers dish towel
berea college crafts sweeper & broom
farmhouse laundry soap
any type of brush
pumice hand soap
true blues ultimate household gloves
twist euro sponge
the mystic mop (a must have!)

hecklewood

streetwear meets workwear

114 northwest third avenue. corner of couch
503.922.1797 www.hecklewood.com
tue - sat 11a - 6p sun noon - 5p

opened in 2006. owner: sam huff
mc. visa
online shopping. gallery

northwest : old town > **s16**

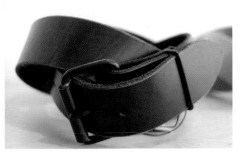

J: This job takes me to a lot of clothing stores—I have had to make a cataloging system to categorize the many different types. For example, there's the "I want to look cool, but I am pushing 40, so can I still get away with this stuff?" place. *Hecklewood* is not so easily pigeonholed. It has a dose of "I need a perfect accessory to top off my already bold look," mixed with "we are super talented craftsmen and make a lot of the stuff right here." It's the cool streetwear meets laidback workwear aesthetic that makes it the right blend for one of my favorite categories: "A must."

covet:
hecklewood:
  pendleton wool hoodies
  scarves
tanner:
  the standard belt
  wallets
  landscape messenger bags

hermitage

bespoke wallpaper and unique housewares

1024 northwest 19th avenue. corner of marshall
503.241.2399 www.hermitagepdx.com
tue - sat 11a - 6p sun - mon by appointment only

opened in 2007. owner: jennifer june
all major credit cards accepted
custom orders

northwest : nob hill > 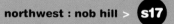 **s17**

J: I was grounded only once as a kid. My parents had just finished hanging bicentennial-themed wallpaper, but I felt the Colonial Williamsburg themes needed some improvements. So I added my John Hancock to the Declaration of Independence. Had the lovely *Hermitage* been around at that time, I may have never gone to such lengths. Here, Jennifer stocks a beautiful collection of tasteful designer wallpapers from small producers along with hand-picked home objects. So when temptation strikes me again to improve on wall décor—now I know where to come to avoid trouble.

covet:
wallpapers:
  erica wakerly
  nana rococo
  hanna werning
paige russell spouts
swedish handcrafted brushes
ostrich egg vases
mairo towels

ink & peat

organic modern floral and lifestyle store

3808 north williams avenue # 126. between beech and failing
503.282.6688 www.inkandpeat.com
tue - sat 11a - 6p sun noon - 5p

opened in 2008. owner: pam zsori
mc. visa
online shopping. registries. custom orders/design. weddings/events

northeast : williams corridor >

K: This past fall and winter have been the grayest and drizzliest on record. Even hardened locals like myself have been feeling the gloom and whining about it like Californians. I feel like if *Ink & Peat's* new space had been opened, people's outlook might have been sunnier—because everybody knows that beautiful flowers can lift a dark mood. And at *Ink & Peat*, gorgeous arrangements and stems are in abundance. Add to that an array of vintage accent pieces and carefully chosen gift and home products, and voila—the rainy day blues will be gone.

covet:
gorgeous arrangements
hable construction pillows
judy jackson pottery
saipua soap & candles
nantaka joy paper products
plover organic linens
oly studio faux bois pieces
lothantique soaps & body care

141

langlitz leather

the haute couture of motorcycle clothing
2443-a southeast division street. between 24th and 25th
503.235.0959 www.langlitz.com
mon - fri 8a - 6p sat by appointment. closed in august

opened in 1947. owner: jackie langlitz hansen and dave hansen
all major credit cards accepted
custom orders

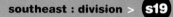
southeast : division > s19

J: Portland may not have a lot of Fortune 500 companies pouring loads o' money into the local economy, but what we do have is way cooler. One example is *Langlitz Leather*. In the world of leather motorcycle garments, *Langlitz's* are considered haute couture. People ride their hogs from around the country to here to get measured for one of *Langlitz's* sweeeeet garments. But a chopper isn't required, just a born-to-be-wild attitude. Boots, belts, chaps, and bags are made right there on the premises. Who needs blue chip when we've got the leather?

covet:
langlitz leather:
  columbia jacket
  cascade jacket
  hard bags
  riding chaps
  biker wallets
  keychains
boots by wesco

life + limb

bringing modern spaces to life

1716 east burnside street. between 17th and 18th
503.233.4738 www.lifeandlimb.net
tue - fri 11a - 6p sat 11a - 5p sun noon - 5p

opened in 2007. owner: molly quan
mc. visa
custom orders / design

northeast : east burnside > **s20**

K: The meaning of *Life + Limb* boils down to continued existence. And one thing we humans need in order to exist are plants—and lots of them. So Molly has created a new style store where the main focus is on indoor plants and succulents and a fresh variety of containers to plant them in. In fact, if you are plant challenged like me, Molly will pot your choices for you. She's so nice. And along with things that grow and keep the earth happy and healthy, Molly offers a smart collection of books and other beautifully designed objects to make earth's inhabitants happy.

covet:
planters of all shapes, sizes & materials
loyal loot log bowls
droog birdhouse
perch! container for one thing
blackstock's collections:
  the drawings of an artistic savant
spitfire girl wood notebooks
menu rubber vases

145

lille boutique

modern romantic lingerie

1007 east burnside. between 10th and 11th
503.232.0333 www.lilleboutique.com
mon by appt. tue - fri 11a - 7p sat noon - 6p sun noon - 5p

opened in 2007. owner: sarah wizemann and sara yurman
all major credit cards accepted
online shopping. custom orders

northeast : east burnside >

K: I love beautiful lingerie, but I don't wear it—I collect it. Both my daughter and my husband conspire to get me to wear pieces from my collection, but alas, it stays tucked away while I trounce around bra-less and wearing non-descript lycra thongs. But walking into *Lille* made me not only want to wear pretty underthings, it made me want to clear out everything I have to make room for the bodalicious-ness here. *Lille* doesn't carry frilly, over-the-top, romance novel lingerie—instead '30s and '40s inspired pieces that are understated yet still gorgeous and feminine. I feel a pretty attack coming on.

covet:
araks
elise aucouturier
the lake & stars
dessous
bodas
princesse tam tam
stella mccartney
vpl

local 35

cool and stylish men's clothing

3556 southeast hawthorne boulevard. corner of 35th place
503.963.8200 www.local35.com
mon - sat 11a - 7p sun 11a - 6p

opened in 2003. owner: justin machus
all major credit cards accepted

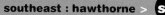

southeast : hawthorne > s22

J: Back in the old days—the early '90s—Portland was working on being cool. There was *Drugstore Cowboy* and Heatmiser, but buying cool men's clothes and shoes was tricky. No more—most folks know that Prada is not a town in Poland, and options for stylish men's (and women's) clothes are good. *Local 35* has done its part bringing us into the '00s in a carefree and elegant way. Stocking both local lines alongside bigger international ones makes this place feel both worldly and local. The future is bright and shiny thanks to *Local 35*.

covet:
nudie jeans
pf flyers
morphine generation
josh podoll
rvca
modern amusement
bblessing
shades of greige

look modern

unsurpassed collection of scandinavian furniture

800 southeast hawthorne. corner of 8th and clay
503.232.5770 www.lookmodern.com
fri - sun 10a - 6p

opened in 2007. owners: connie and les castile
mc. visa
online shopping. custom orders

southeast : industrial >

J: Does Denmark have theme parks? *Look Modern* could easily be renamed *Teakland* or *Six Flags of Denmark over Hawthorne*. In a large second floor warehouse space, hearts race at the unsurpassed selection of Scandinavian designers like Saarinen, Jacobsen, and my personal favorite Morgensen. Les and Connie are the grand masters overseeing all of this beauty that mostly comes from Scandinavia and arrives in shipments every few months. If you need a swanky couch or sleek dining room table there is no need to look elsewhere, *Look Modern*.

covet:
borge morgensen brown leather couch
notsjo vase
arne vodder credenza
hans wegner sofa set
taccia lamp
le corbusier lounge
palaset storage system
ernest sohn cheese board

madison park

antiques with a story
7805 southeast 13th avenue. corner of lambert
503.233.3731 www.madisonparkantiques.com
tue - sat 11a - 6p sun noon - 5p mon by appointment only

opened in 2007. owners: diana leitner, randy parman and donna cedergreen
all major credit cards accepted

southeast : sellwood > 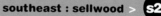 **s24**

K: When I was growing up, my mother used to take my brother and me antiquing all the time. There was lots of grousing on our side and plenty of yawning. But that was then, and this is now—going to antique stores these days is an activity to look forward to, especially if heading to *Madison Park*. Coming here is like finding oneself in a Victorian or Edwardian snapshot. Diana, Donna and Randy have exquisite taste and are master visual storytellers. Each step is a new vignette to explore, and rumour has it that Christmas here is not to be missed. So I won't.

covet:
vintage:
  christening gowns & baby dresses
  ladie's shoes
  rosaries
  french ivory celluloid
  apothecary bottles
  fels-naptha soap
  assorted curiosities

odessa

410 southwest 13th avenue. between burnside and washington
503.223.1998 www.odessaboutique.com
mon - sat 11a - 7p

opened in 2006. owner: susan tompkins
all major credit cards accepted

southwest : west end > **s25**

J: When Susan first opened *Odessa* in the Pearl District 12 years ago, woman's clothing here consisted of hers and that of a *St. Johns* store downtown. Okay, I exaggerate to make the point that Susan has been teaching, informing and gently prodding women of style here for a long time, and she continues to do so from her store in the West End. As Portland has grown, so has *Odessa*. For the ultra-stylish woman who wants to look modern and sophisticated, this is an essential place to shop. And for the ladies who embrace Chanel light, *St. Johns* is still downtown.

covet:
a.f. vandevorst
jane mayle
acne jeans
coming soon by yohji yamamoto
kerry cassill textiles
isabel marant
shipley & halmos
hoss intropia

office pdx

quality products for the modern worker

2204 northeast alberta street. corner of 22nd
888.355.SHOP(7467) www.officepdx.com
tue - fri 11a - 6p sat 11a - 5p sun 11a - 4p

opened in 2005. owners: kelly coller and tony secolo
all major credit cards accepted
online shopping. events

northeast : alberta > 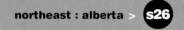 **s26**

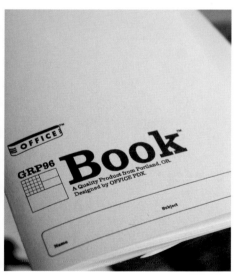

K: There are certain people and certain places that communities seem to swirl around. In Portland (and well beyond), Tony and Kelly and their swellerific store *Office PDX* are very epi (as in epi-center). This is not just happenstance, but the byproduct of a hard-working couple who really understand what jingles the creatives jangles: everything from the best portfolios in town, to smartly curated shows and events, to their own line of office and paper products. Did I hear paper products? Roll up the doors and I'll just back up the car to load.

covet:
office pdx brand "office" supplies:
  grp96 notebook
  olivetti print
vintage typewriters
randoseru japanese school bags
hammerpress letterpress cards & notebooks
pina zangaro everything!
haeger panther

olio united

story-driven clothing, houseware and gifts for women, men and kids

1028 southeast water avenue, suite 120. between yamhill and taylor
503.542.5000 www.oliounited.com
mon - sat 10a - 6p

opened in 2007. owners: cathy mcmurray and korinne james
all major credit cards accepted
online shopping. custom orders

southeast : industrial >

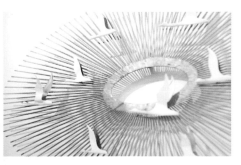

K: For the longest time I thought that *Olio United* was called *Oreo United*. So while browsing the racks here, I was secretly looking for snack foods. Sadly, there were none to be found, but I did find not one, not two, but three pairs of shoes that made me much happier than Oreos ever could. In fact, everywhere I looked here there were wonderful items, from women's and men's clothing to kids'—and a super fresh assortment of paper products and such. And what makes this place even more delectable is that local, green and sustainable are key to *Olio's* belief system. Looks good—is good!

covet:
preloved
prairie underground
paper doll
good society denim
jack & marjorie bags
melissa shoes
fig kids clothing
prismera jewelry

pinkham millinery

handmade hats for men and women

515 southwest broadway in morgan's alley. between washington and alder
503.796.9385 www.pinkhammillinery.com
wed - sat 11a - 5:30p tue by appointment

opened in 2000. owner: dayna pinkham
mc. visa
online shopping. custom orders

southwest : downtown > **s28**

J: There are many great hat moments in television and movie history. Think Sophia Loren's enormous brimmed red number in *Prêt-à-Porter*. Or Indiana Jone's fedora. Owner of *Pinkham Millinery*, Dayna, understands the importance of the well made exclamation point for your head. Trained in classical European millinery, she exquisitely builds each and every hat in her atelier. After a meeting, gathering your measurements and needs, she will make a special hat for any occasion that requires a little extra drama. Or an everyday cap for your Mary Tyler Moore, new-girl-in-town performance.

covet:
pinkham millinery:
  collapsible fedora
  toque perch
  etched peacock perch
  sloper fedora
  lace-up cloche
  top-stitched fedora
  adams cap

popina

fresh retro swimwear and more

4831 northeast 42nd avenue. corner of alberta court
503.282.5159 www.popinaswim.com
see hours on website

opened in 2006. owner: pamela levenson
mc. visa
online shopping. custom orders

northeast : beaumont/wilshire > **s29**

K: Everybody dreads shopping for swimsuits. Most women I know put it on a par with going to the dentist. Why is this? When you wear a swimsuit, you're usually doing something fun, and while you might be sporting an Oregon tan (blue/white skin), with the right suit, you'll be a stunner! And the right suit is sure to be found at *Popina*. Pamela's designs are retro in feel and make every figure look great. Choose from what she's got in store (or online), and if it needs a few custom alterations for the perfect fit, no problem, her staff is on it! See ladies? Swimsuits are your friend!

covet:
popina suits:
  retro halter
  drawcord bottom
  wendy tankini
  swimsuit skirts
havaiana slims
two loops beach bags
speedo flower cap

relish

thoughtfully designed products that tell a story

1715 northwest lovejoy street. between 17th and 18th
503.227.3779 www.shoprelish.com
tue - sat 11a - 6p mon by appointment only

opened in 2001. owner: trisha guido
all major credit cards accepted
online shopping. custom registries
design services / product sourcing custom orders / design

northwest : lower nob hill > **s30**

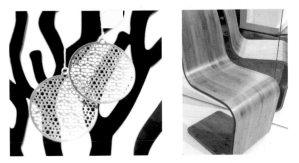

K: When it comes to condiments, relish seems key to me. Ketchup is just sweetened tomato sauce and mustard, when of the yellow variety, is bo-ring. But relish has got personality, it's got texture, it's got verve! And *Relish,* the store, has all of these qualities, too! Now that it has moved to its gorgeous and spacious new space, Trisha has the room to really show her stuff. And it's all very good stuff indeed—ranging from furniture to jewelry to textiles—everything is carefully chosen for its high craft and modern simplicity. You'll never take relish for granted again.

covet:
designer's eye textiles
polli jewelry
rosenthal dinnerware
design house stockholm
unison bedding
marimekko everything
sophie cook bottles
custom textile fabrications

scrap

school and community reuse action project

3901a north williams avenue. between failing and shaver
503.294.0769 www.scrapaction.org
wed 11a - 8p thu - sat 11a - 5p

opened in 1998
all major credit cards accepted
summer camp. membership

north : williams corridor > **s31**

J: There is no crap at *Scrap*. At this nonprofit, you'll find surplus office, industrial and who-knows-what supplies being resold with the intention of being used again as arts-and-craft materials. All it takes is a little creativity. I recently saw an old bowling trophy, which could be turned into a scale model replica and cake topper of the Glisan turnaround with its shiny Joan of Arc statue. Or what about the box full of old dentures? No problem-o. I will hand these out at Halloween as a reminder to brush often after massive candy consumption. You see, making something cool at *Scrap* is a snap.

covet:
old stock onion-skin paper
glittery alphabet stickers
model teeth
cool snaps
stamp-making kits
picture frames
needlepoint materials
cool scalloped blue placemats

spielwerk

simple toys lead to extraordinary ideas

7956 southeast 13th avenue. between miller and nehalem
503.736.3000 www.spielwerk.net
mon - sat 10a - 6p sun 11a - 5p

opened in 2006. owners: sonja barclay and stacee wion
mc. visa
online shopping. custom orders. wish lists. classes

southeast : sellwood >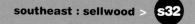

K: If I knew that in the blink of an eye I would go from ten years old, swinging in a tire swing in my backyard and building roly-poly habitats, to being a slightly frazzled travel-guide publisher—I would have tried to squeeze more play out of my childhood. Of course I wouldn't have had *Spielwerk* back then, with its cool toys that will inspire endless hours of play in not just kids but also in their parents who, like me, are more than happy to turn back the clock a bit (or a lot) and throw themselves into the joy of play.

covet:
skuut bikes
labyrinth balance boards
great arts & crafts supplies
kidsonroof cardboard house
kraul physics toys
anchor hand-cut stone blocks
games! games! games!
doll clothing by local seamstresses

stand up comedy

forward-fashion boutique

811 east burnside street. corner of eighth
503.233.3382 www.shopstandingup.us
tue - sat 11a - 7p sun noon - 6p

opened in 2007. owners: rachel silberstein and diana kim
mc. visa
online shopping. custom orders. gallery

northeast : east burnside >

J: Have I ever told you the one about the two girls who met in tap-dancing class in Minneapolis? In between a barrel turn and a lindy hop, Diana and Rachel were struck by each other's sophisticated styles. After becoming fast friends and relocating to Portland, they opened the forward fashion shop, *Stand Up Comedy*. Here they specialize in super chic designers like Bless, Staerk and Henrik Vibskov. They also feature cool art objects. So what's the punchline? Here it comes... the two were dapper tappers. Ba-dum-bump.

covet:
slow and steady wins the race
bless
ann-sofie back
pelican avenue
arielle de pinto jewelry
acne jeans
rachel comey shoes
stepanie dearmond sculptures

171

ste. maine

home furnishings, exquisite objects and design studio

1626 southeast bybee boulevard. near corner of milwaukie
503.232.1880 www.saintmaine.com
mon - sat 10a - 6p sun noon - 4p

opened in 2008. owners: erin and elizabeth manwaring
all major credit cards accepted
online shopping. registries. custom orders/design

southeast : westmoreland >

K: Exquisite is a hard word to live up to. But if there's a home design store in Portland that can live up to this word, *Ste. Maine* can. Walking in here is transformative, where the world around you which just moments before was mundane and chaotic, turns into glamorous and serene. I didn't know where to look first: the enticing array of art books, or the *Ste. Maine* dinnerware which is both stunning to look at and stunningly low priced. Erin and Elizabeth are talented with a capital T, and if you want a bit of their magic to rub off on you and onto your home, I suggest a visit asap.

covet:
ste. maine designs:
  upholstered pieces
  pillows
  dinnerware
  paper goods
michael manwaring art
oromono seabloom throw
amazing design/art book selection

sunlan

any light bulb you would ever want

3901 north mississippi avenue. corner of failing
503.281.0453 www.sunlanlighting.com
mon - fri 8a - 5:30p sat 10a - 5p

opened in 1990. owner: kay newell
mc. visa
special orders

north : mississippi > 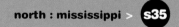 **s35**

J: Keep Portland weird! Hell, yeah, we love our cast of strange characters that makes Portland unique. If it is not packs of ne'er-do-wells riding towering bicycle contraptions, then it is our collection of awesome, funky shops with eccentric themes. Need a rock? *Ed's House of Gems*. A lightbulb? *Sunlan* it is. There is so much more here than at the light bulb aisle at *Fred Meyer*. This is where you go to buy bulbs of distinction. From antique reproduction bulbs to LED strands of Christmas lights, *Sunlan* is one big light therapy spot that keeps Portland glowing.

covet:
happy light therapy lights
perma-glow bulbs
flicker flame bulbs
fiber optic butterfly nightlight
lamp making supplies
christmas lights
barge lights
rainbow party bulbs

the perfume house

amazing collection of european and american perfumes

3328 southeast hawthorne boulevard. between 33rd and 34th
503.234.5375 www.theperfumehouse.com
summer hours tue - fri 10a - 6p sat - sun 10a - 5p
winter hours mon - fri 10a - 6p sat 10a - 5p

opened in 1979. owner: chris tsefalas
all major credit cards accepted
online shopping. custom orders

southeast : hawthorne > **s36**

J: I don't suggest following your nose to *The Perfume House*, which is arguably the most comprehensive and important collection of perfumes in the country. You might lose your way here as winds of patchouli and sage scents blow strong in the Hawthorne district where this mecca is located. Chris is a bona fide trained nose—his expertise is so revered that people make special trips to Portland to meet with this olfactory oracle in hopes of finding a signature perfume. During your appointment, he will help you find the special fragrance that says you. And hopefully that ain't Charlie.

covet:
annick goutal
henry jacques
sabi
rancè
clive christian
hermès
acqua di parma
caron

tilde

accents for body and home

7919 southeast 13th avenue. corner of lexington
503.234.9600 www.tildeshop.com
tue - sat 10a - 6p sun noon - 5p

opened in 2006. owner: debbe hamada
mc. visa
online shopping. registries

southeast : sellwood > **s37**

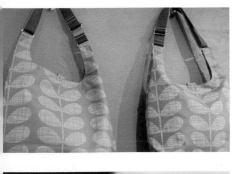

K: I've decided recently that I need a vivaciousness refresher course. Seems they don't offer that class at Portland State, so I'm going to the University of *Tilde* where Debbe is going to not only let me soak up the rays of her sunny personality but also be surrounded by the vibrant goods in her store. This is a go-to spot to find great gifts. You'll feel good buying here as well as giving—because many items are designed and made by locals or by smallish companies that are craft oriented. You'll feel sprightlier just by walking through the door at *Tilde*.

covet:
modern twist hide box
leah nobilette spiky bowls
orla kiely bags & wallets
crystalyn kae bags
obi design belts
satsuma press letterpress cards
etui prints & cards
shoshana snow ceramics

una

eclectic collection of exquisite clothes and accessories

2802 southeast ankeny street. corner of 28th
503.235.2326 www.una-myheartisfull.com
tue - sun 11a - 6p

opened in 2005. owner: giovanna parolari
mc. visa
custom orders

**northeast : east burnside > **

J: Bird watchers spend their lives trying to catch a glimpse of a red-naped sapsucker. I have friends who watch for stylish girls with the same fervor. They will excitedly call one another with the news of "a girl in hot pink pumps, a navy silk trench dress with three-quarter puff sleeves." These friends should hang outside of *Una*, where the migratory habits of Portland's most stylish come to confer with Giovanna. Here she's built an intimate nest of smart, stylish clothing. That and the well appointed collection of ceramics and accessories helps make *Una* celestial.

covet:
sunshine & shadow
rodebjer
malene birger
schiesser
tom scott
m/m masayuki marukawa
alice park wallets
melissa joy manning

veloshop

awesome bike and accessory shop
211 southwest ninth avenue. between burnside and oak
503.335.8356 www.veloshop.org
mon - fri 10a - 6p sat noon - 5p

opened in 2003. owner: molly cameron
mc. visa
custom orders

southwest : west end > **s39**

J: I often suffer from a reality-and-dream-world dis-connect. You see, in real life I ride a 14-year-old burnt-copper-colored-mountain bike. It's functional and heavy and no one will ever steal it. But in my mind I ride a kelly green, custom-built, fixed-gear bike with bright yellow rims. To escape to my fantasy world I sometimes pop in and visit *Veloshop* where they have all the bike parts and the other stuff that I own in my fake, fantasy world. They are so nice here—they play along with my delusions and they don't laugh as I jump on my clunky Huffy and squeak away.

covet:
honjo fenders
dugast tubular tires
full wood fenders
huge selection of colored rims
r. e. load messenger bag
chamois creme
custom bike fit service
fmb tires

why not?

vintage treasures and reproductions

8315 southeast 13th avenue. between umatilla and harney
503.542.2577 www.whynotcollections.com
tue - sat 11a - 5p sometimes open sun

opened in 2007. owner: shelley henkle
mc. visa
custom orders / design

southeast : sellwood > 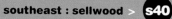 **s40**

K: I am a modernist. I like clean, graphic lines and tend toward minimalism. Wait, this is the fantasy me! The real me lives in a 1912 house with antiques and has a secret thing for gingham. Therefore the real me was totally tickled when I happened upon *Why Not?* Shelley has created a world that evokes Dorothy and Toto and the Boxcar Children, of lunches packed in pails and pigtails tied with bright red ribbon. I found myself drawn especially to Shelley's creations like the re-imagined children's clothing and bibs made from old dishclothes.

covet:
why not? designs
antique doll beds & children's furniture
l'amour t-straps
vintage books
juivel baby blankets
glitter houses
sherrie waik scrapbooks
little golden books

xtabay vintage

glamorous vintage clothing
2515 southeast clinton. between 25th and 26th
503.230.2899 www.xtabayvintage.blogspot.com
thu noon - 6p fri noon - 7p sat - tue noon - 6p

opened in 2001. owner: liz gross
mc. visa
private shopping parties

southeast : clinton > **s41**

J: Some cities are great for finding vintage clothing and some aren't. For example, a city like Paris surprisingly is not good for finding vintage. The French seem to want to put vintage in a museum rather than on their bodies. But if the frogs came here for a visit, they would see what dipping into the past could offer. This is a quintessential vintage clothing city. At *Xtabay*, the French would realize that an incredible offering of vintage ladies' clothing can span many eras while still looking incredibly contemporary and fresh. Poor Parisians—at least they still have their croissants.

covet:
perfect '40s navy pencil skirt
new, old jantzen wrap skirt
cute '60s cocktail dresses
charles f. berg fuschia jacket
lacoste coral polo shirt dress
variety red & white striped knit cotton tee
jewel tone '70s netted gold block heels
'70s rainbow pleated skirt

notes

Everett Street Bistro (14th + Everett)

notes

etc.

the eat.shop guides were created by kaie wellman and are published by cabazon books

for more information about the series, or to buy print or online books, please visit: eatshopguides.com

eat.shop portland 5th edition was written, researched and photographed by kaie wellman and jon hart

editing: kaie wellman   copy editing: lynn king   fact checking: emily mattson
map and layout production: julia dickey addition photography: lola de garmo

kaie thx jon. jon thx kaie.

cabazon books: eat.shop portland 5th edition
ISBN-13 978-0-9799557-5-4

every effort has been made to ensure the accuracy of the information in this book. however, certain details
are subject to change. please remember when using the guides that hours alter seasonally and sometimes
sadly, businesses close. the publisher cannot accept responsibility for any consequences arising from the
use of this book.

the eat.shop guides are distributed by independent publishers group: www.ipgbook.com